I am Ndileka

I am Ndileka
More than my surname

Ndileka Mandela

First published by Jacana Media (Pty) Ltd in 2019

10 Orange Street
Sunnyside
Auckland Park 2092
South Africa
+2711 628 3200
www.jacana.co.za

© Ndileka Mandela, 2019

All rights reserved.

ISBN 978-1-4314-2906-6

Cover design by T
Layout by Alexandra Turner
Editing by Linda Da Nova
Proofreading by Lara Jacob
Set in Sabon 11/16pt
Printed by ABC Press
Job no. 003594

See a complete list of Jacana titles at www.jacana.co.za

Dedicated to my mother

In every candle lit,

The Mthembu woman rises,

In the spirit of uThembekile

And in the memory of Thokozile,

As she walks, these are the steps of a Soldier in the making

'Cause in every touch there is quality in her

The constant elegance that is her,

To change humanity

It's that wisdom, the art of the Afrocentric Queen, of whom I speak,

Preach of her independence,

That is truly divine, in the life and times of Ms Ndi,

'Cause in every lesson, there is a spark of her

Knowledge, which will be pasted

With that light of her spark for the next Generation to come,

Mama I SALUTE you because your work has just begun in society

Long live NDI, Long live

Tembela Mandela

Contents

Foreword ix
Prologue. xii

Part One
Birth and childhood 3
Boarding school 22
Family 33

Part Two
My father. 41
Madiba, my grandfather 52
Evelyn, my grandmother 78
Ouma, my maternal grandmother 93

Part Three
Motherhood. 99
The importance of education 116
Dealing with death. 125
Relationships 143

Part Four
Expectations and challenges of being a Mandela 157
Being homeless 169
Depression 175
Being a woman in South Africa today 185
The caregiver 209

Part Five
Finding my voice 217
Finding my passion 221

Conclusion 237
Acknowledgements 243

Foreword

Ndileka ... a name meaning Dignity...

NDILEKA MANDELA, THE FIRST OF the First of the First ... the first child of Thembekile Mandela, the firstborn of Nelson Mandela from his first wife, Evelyn Mase Mandela. Born as the first in the next generation of the Mandela lineage, born to take the lead, Ndileka's leadership is evident in her role as a social activist and in continuing the legacy of her grandfather, Nelson Mandela, while carving out her own unique legacy.

The world watched as Ndileka became the first Mandela to publicly make a stand to hold our leaders accountable, to be a voice for the people, a moral conscience to remind our leaders and the people of our nation to lead, to live and to act in alignment with the values of her granddad and the founding mothers and fathers of our glorious nation and our democracy as enshrined in the Freedom Charter and the Constitution.

I have been fortunate to walk this journey with Sis Ndi, as I fondly call her. Our journey together began nine years ago when we met while raising support to build the Nelson Mandela Children's Hospital – one of her granddad's last projects. Sis Ndi shares her granddad's love for children and healthcare, coming from her medical background as an ICU nurse by profession. I would often remark that the world is in need of intensive care and would express gratitude for her tireless efforts in contributing to the spiritual, moral, mental and emotional wellbeing of society and the world at large.

During this time, serving with Sis Ndi in my role as Chief Operating Officer of the Thembekile Mandela Foundation and Director of the Leading Like Mandela leadership development programme, I have watched her develop and unleash her personal greatness as she continues to rise as a daughter of the African soil while dealing with personal difficulties and finding solutions for the common challenges that we face as Africans.

I watched with hope and pride as she established the Thembekile Mandela Foundation to honour her father and to continue the legacy of her granddad in striving to improve the quality of education and healthcare in South Africa and the continent, two pillars Nelson Mandela stated were essential to build our nation.

I have watched as she launched Pride of the Rural Girl, an initiative to recognise and restore the pride and dignity of the rural girl child; being raised as a girl child in the rural Eastern Cape, she understands their plight. I watched, after we drove at the crack of dawn to a rural village, as Sis Ndi, in jeans and a T-shirt, took a spade and shovelled wheelbarrow after wheelbarrow of plaster to build classrooms for a rural school. She addressed the community on the importance of playing an active role in their own development and the future of their children, played hopscotch and skipped with the schoolchildren, showered the kids with affectionate hugs and stories of her granddad and watched their smiles as she inspired them to study and to shine like the brightest stars in the galaxy.

I joined her in celebrating her success as she launched Leading Like Mandela with Ms Amina Mohammed, the Deputy Secretary-General of the United Nations, and other esteemed dignitaries to support the development of effective leadership on the continent amongst the youth and current leaders.

In this time I have also been able to observe Sis Ndi graciously fulfilling her various roles as a daughter, continuing the memory of her father; as a granddaughter, taking a sabbatical for three years to be by her granddad's side during his last years; her role and efforts in securing him a fitting burial and continuing his legacy, a legacy that he sacrificed his life for; as a mother, dealing with daily responsibilities such as shopping for groceries, cooking a meal for her kids, confirming travel arrangements for her daughter at university; as a grandmother to Nabeela, singing along to Barney tunes while reviewing and keeping abreast of the latest news and political and social developments in the country and further afield; discussing and preparing for media interviews and meetings with world leaders, presidents and royalty; and as I leave, coming to greet me in the driveway and praising the gardener for the beautiful roses that are in bloom – glimpses of her personal and professional life that you will discover in this book.

When I was approached by Ndileka to write this foreword to her memoir, the first thought that entered my mind was, 'Where does one begin? Where do I begin to share insights on the life of a truly great leader and daughter of Africa, a human of such nobility, dignity and greatness, an enigma? A daughter who has paid the huge price of a childhood in the rural Eastern Cape without a father, during the days of apartheid, and robbed of the presence of her grandfather.'

Where does one begin to paint a portrait of a person, to introduce her memoir to the world, which takes the reader on a journey into her life growing up in the era of apartheid, raised by her grandmother Evelyn? A journey of personal strife and challenges as an individual and as a member of one of the world's most renowned and respected families, and a journey towards becoming a social activist, reminding us to hold our heads high and to live with dignity as Africans, to remember the spirit of ubuntu, to continue the long walk to freedom, to honour and to liberate ourselves from the shackles of our hearts and minds just as her granddad led the struggle of our people to liberate us from the shackles of apartheid. This long-awaited memoir grants deeper insights and a greater understanding into the life of Ndileka Mandela, much more than her surname.

Liaqat Alli Azam
Director, Leading Like Mandela

Prologue

Being Ndileka and more than just my surname

I AM NDILEKA MANDELA. FIRSTBORN child of Thembekile Madiba Mandela and first grandchild of Nelson Rolihlahla Mandela.

For a large portion of my life, I have felt invisible to the broader public as an individual simply because I carry the last name of one of the world's most beloved icons.

This feeling of invisibility, I believe, has been compounded by being almost cast out of the personal history of this great man, uTata, as he's affectionately known by South Africans. A single narrative prevails, one that leaves out chunks of his life, particularly his marriage to his first wife, Evelyn Nomathamsanqa Mandela, and that of my father, Thembekile.

In September 2010, I was picking up my daughter, Pumla, who had spent a weekend at a friend's house. Usually I'd wait outside and send her a text to meet me upon my arrival. On this occasion, she came out to tell me that her friend's mother wanted to meet me. Just to get acquainted.

I went in and was met by a cheerful and sociable lady named Tembeka. After exchanging pleasantries, she proceeded to ask me what I was doing workwise at that point. I started fretting and told her the three-year RDP housing project I'd been coordinating had come to an end, and I was at a loss as to what I wanted to do next.

In fact, this project was meant to have run for only 18 months but since my contract was to last until its completion, the company had retained my services.

One thing I knew then was that I did not want to be employed any longer; I wanted to be self-employed. I was 45 years old at this point.

What she said next changed my life irrevocably.

She said, "I don't know what your problem is. You are the first of the first of the first."

"Huh?" I asked out of slight confusion.

She explained to me that I was the first grandchild (not granddaughter – grandchild, period) of Nelson Rolihlahla Mandela from his firstborn, Thembekile Madiba Mandela, from his first wife, Evelyn Nomathamsanqa Mandela.

In the course of my life, I have found out that this comes with responsibilities. More about that later.

At this point, I think it's safe to assume you want to know why I have decided to write this book. I write for myriad reasons, my main motivator being my desire to share the experiences of my journey through life. People have attributed my character to my grandfather and I'm writing to tell all who believe this, it is not so. I also believe that my story or journey, as it were, is intertwined with the missing parts of the story of my grandfather, which I feel is not complete.

All books that have been written about him are about a politician, an icon, a liberator and other illustrious descriptions that are used to describe him. The other side of him as a human being, a husband, a father, a grandfather, an uncle and a brother are missing. Granted, this other side appears sporadically in most literature written about him, but not in detail. My intention is to therefore use my story to fill some of these gaps.

For instance, my father is but a smudge in his life. He is the son who died in a car accident at age 24, leaving behind a young widow with two small children, my sister, Nandi, and me.

While Granddad was imprisoned with his comrades, his children had to flee being targeted by the police. My father and his siblings went to study in Swaziland and that is where my parents met. He studied at St Christopher's School for Boys and my mother, Thoko Nkosi, at St Theresa's, which was a girls' school. Uncle Matoto told me they met during sports day at St Theresa's. It was a sister school to St Christopher's and it is there where my parents' whirlwind romance began. I am also told they made a smashing couple, as both were quite tall.

I was raised by my grandmother, Evelyn Nomathamsanqa Mandela (whom I called Rundu, a pet name because I could not say Nkgono, which was what our Sesotho-speaking neighbours called her in Orlando East) and lived with her until I birthed my firstborn, Tembela. I suppose this was because I was her first grandchild. I never really asked her why I stayed with her. It could also have been because my parents were still young, both in their early twenties at the time. Perhaps Rundu felt more equipped to raise me. What I know for a fact is that it was the best decision they made for me because a large part of my makeup is due to Evelyn Nomathamsanqa Mandela's influence.

I've mentioned how my character or who I have become

is always attributed to Granddad and how that is not true. In all the interviews I have ever granted, the bulk of the interview has been about Granddad. Over time this has presented a challenge for me, as it shows a narrow view of who I am, what drives me and what is behind the decisions I have made and continue to make.

Often when I have shared titbits of my life on social media, my followers, or what I call my public family, have always asked me when I will write my story. I am not only writing for them but for me as well. I have found that as the years go by, there are certain parts of your life that seem to get lost as they aren't documented. There are parts of my life that I want to make better sense of and, by having them down in black and white, I can finally achieve it.

I want to confront some of my ghosts through this book and finally lay them to rest. Contrary to popular belief, people think being from this family is a walk in the park and that we perhaps do not go through the same challenges as everyone else. My life has been a labyrinth of highs and lows and I'm still standing. I thank God for that and my ancestors for all their intercessions.

I am the sum of all the decisions I have made so far, good and bad.

I am Ndileka Mandela, the First of the First of the First, and this is my story.

Part One

Chapter 1

Birth and childhood

I DO NOT KNOW WHETHER I was born in Cape Town or Johannesburg. I do, however, know that my date of birth is 22 February 1965.

My early childhood days were spent in Orlando East, 5818 Mashane Street, in a typical four-roomed council house. The kind that for the longest time was the norm in Soweto. These houses had two rooms you could use as bedrooms, one as a dining room and one as a kitchen. They had no bathrooms. We bathed in the kitchen in big enamel basins with hot water boiled from a coal stove. There were no toilets inside the houses. Our toilet was situated in the corner of the backyard. These were old-school toilets where the cistern was placed high above the toilet bowl to assist the water to flow gravitationally. I used to have to be accompanied to this toilet, as I could not flush it on my own.

In our backyard, we had peach trees and Rundu, my grandmother, would make canned fruit out of them. I loved watching and assisting her. Well, more like sampling tastes of the sweet syrupy mixture she used to preserve the peaches. In the front yard, we had grape vines, but the grapes they produced were always sour.

My earliest childhood memories date back to when I was a toddler. I am sitting on my grandmother's lap in the kitchen and Rundu's sister, Granny Kate, who lived in Mzimhlophe, is making a fire in the coal stove. Granny Kate was married to Mr Mgudlwa, and her eldest daughter, Aunt Lulama, years later would open and co-own a shop in Cofimvaba with Rundu.

The stove was a greenish cream colour. In this memory, I am drinking from my bottle. The mere fact that I can remember this memory and its finer details suggests to me that I was too old to be drinking from a bottle. '*Bengiyingudu*', where '*ngudu*' in this context is a colloquial term for a person that has come of age.

Now Rundu's sister must have been sick and tired of this *ngudu* still drinking from a baby bottle because without warning she yanked the bottle out of my mouth and threw it in the fire. Of course, I screamed in protest. Now that I think of it as I write this, it must have been all part of the plan, as I believe that Rundu did not have the heart to wean me off the bottle.

I also remember that I used to attend a crèche in Orlando where Rundu would drop me off on her way to Pimville Clinic, where she worked as a community nurse. Aunt Maki, who is my father's sister and Rundu's last born, would pick me up on her way back from school on most afternoons. She was a learner at Orlando High School and one of her teachers was Mr Tamsanqa Kambule. Uncle Makgatho, who was my father's younger brother, also lived with us in Orlando. Even in my early childhood memories, Uncle Kgatho (short for Makgatho) was always very loving and quiet.

I have to say, Rundu spoilt me rotten. During school

holidays I would stay home with my Aunt Maki. If I was naughty, which was often the case, she would give me a hiding. I would then sulk for most of the day until I knew Rundu would be coming home. There was a street that ran perpendicular to Mashane Street and our house was the second house from the corner house, which was owned by Mr Mavuka. He owned a shop not far from our home. The minute I spotted Rundu in her green nurse's uniform, I would start screaming as if my aunt had just spanked me. Rundu would run down the street and shout at my aunt.

'*Makaziwe, umenza ntoni umntana wam?*' she'd shout. (Makaziwe, what are you doing to my child?) Hearing this gave me immense joy. I would have a smirk and a glint in my eye, as I knew it would be a while before she laid her hands on me again.

When I was around six years old, I began to be allowed to accompany Rundu to the clinic, where she was on half-day duty. I guess that is how the seed of nursing as a career choice was planted in me. I would assist her with small tasks like moving the weights when she weighed babies who came in with their mothers for consultation. If the child's weight matched their percentile growth – a term I now know since becoming a community nurse like her – the mother would be given sugar-coated jelly jubes. This was exclusively my job and I would help myself to one every time I put these in a small brown paper packet. Mind you, I would keep a stash for myself as TTO (treatment taken out) for when I went home later. I ate so many sweets that I do not remember my milk teeth falling out on their own. They were so rotten, I had to visit the dentist frequently to take them out.

Besides the dental visits, there was another price to be paid for eating so many sweets. Every alternate Saturday, first thing in the morning, it was castor oil time. Rundu would warm it, mix it with freshly squeezed orange juice and then it would be time to gobble the concoction and get ready to *ukukhupha inyongo*. Nowadays it's called detoxing. I hated this fortnightly ritual with a passion. But do you think it deterred me from eating sweets? Never!

I attended Sub A and B at Zakheni Primary School in Orlando. During the week, we would take a commuter taxi – a valiant Six Mabone, as we called them, owing to the six taillights they had. The taxi would drop me off on the same street where Zakheni was located – that's how safe it was in those days; there was no worry that harm would befall me – while Rundu stayed on the taxi, getting off at the Orlando Station where she would then take the commuter train to the clinic.

One day, as we were getting into the taxi, the car door slammed onto my fingers. I cried all the way to my drop-off point but by the time I reached school I had stopped crying. Shortly before assembly started, guess who walked from Orlando Station to kiss my sore hand better and give me more lunch money? Rundu of course. She used to give me 5c, which would buy me a quarter loaf of white bread, *isishebo* and atchar. That day I was Ms Moneybags with 10c, and I splurged on sausages and an ice lolly. In 1971 our version of an ice lolly was sweetened, frozen Kool Aid in small plastic sandwich bags.

This reminds of how entrepreneurial I was as a preteen. During school holidays, I used to sell Kool Aid ice blocks and by the time school reopened I would be Ms Moneybags again. This money came in very handy during the school excursions Zakheni used to have. We would go to either Pretoria or Johannesburg Zoo. I loved these excursions, as we would have a big picnic at the zoo. What I liked most was that Rundu would really go to town for these excursions, with roasted chicken sandwiches and sweets, of course, and

I could hand these out as I wished.

One time, Ms Dlova, our Sub A teacher, announced that we would visit Pretoria Zoo just after the Easter break. The price of this excursion was R10. Rundu gave me this amount that night to give to Ms Dlova the next day at school. Upon seeing that no one else had been given the money for the excursion yet, I decided to wait a little longer before handing it over to our teacher. Guess what I did during the break? I splurged and entertained my close friends. I figured I would have enough time to recoup the costs by selling ice blocks during the Easter weekend. I never thought Aunt Maki would decide to defrost the fridge that Saturday, which was peak time to sell my Kool Aid ice blocks. You see, Sunday was church day and my friends would not be able to come and purchase.

The Tuesday after the Easter weekend came, and the excursion was planned for that Friday. I knew I was screwed, but I could not tell Rundu about my splurge. I was in agony all by myself. It was my little secret. During the week, I kept trying to feign illness. No matter how hard I tried, it did not work. Thursday arrived, and I watched Rundu preparing sandwiches for my excursion. By the time Friday rolled around, I had devised a plan. I was just going to sit outside the school until the buses came back. Morning assembly took place as usual and, as is customary, each class teacher called out the names of pupils who had paid for the excursion to stand on one side. Ms Dlova did so for her class and only a few of us remained. When Ms Dlova was not paying attention and all the other pupils were excitedly clamouring for the buses, I sneaked onto the bus, hoping no pupil noticed, and made sure I sat right at the back. I was very wrong. One Gqatsa Fly, a busy body, saw. She kept screaming that I had to get out off the bus, as I did not pay. Thankfully, I was rescued by one of the friends I had splurged on, who gave her dirty looks to silence her. I couldn't wait for the buses to start moving. All things considered, this excursion turned out to be the best, as I had the pocket money to spend that Rundu had given me along with the sandwiches.

December of 1971 holds another fond memory for me. This time, it is of a trip we made by train. My mother, Thoko, had been living in Cape Town. Dad had been buried two years prior to this visit.

I was to visit my mother in Cape Town, chaperoned by Aunt Maki. It would be my first time on a train. The journey would take us two days from Park Station to Cape Town Station. I remember the night before we were to board the train, I could not sleep out of excitement. Aunt Maki and I shared a room. I kept waking her up almost every two hours with the same question: '*Sihamba nini?*' (When are we leaving?) By the time morning came, she was not just exhausted but fed up with me too. Rundu accompanied us by taxi to Park Station. She and Aunt Maki checked the board to see which platform our train would be departing from and at what time it would come through. After checking, we went to the assigned platform to wait for the train.

When the train came, both Rundu and Aunty checked which coach was allocated to us. We were on the second-class coach, which was grand. I can't remember if we shared it with other people or not. All I remember is the goodies that we were going to eat on the train, packed neatly in a locked picnic basket. Rundu helped us settle and then a whistle blew to warn all those accompanying the passengers that it was time to bid their goodbyes, as the train was about to leave. After the third whistle, Rundu got off the train. Very shortly, the train started moving away from the platform. We stood in the corridor next to our sleeping compartment as Rundu waved her white handkerchief, bidding us a customary safe journey. We stood at the window as she grew smaller and smaller until we could hardly see her. I was beside myself with excitement at this adventure. Aunty gave me some fruit and when nighttime came, a train steward gave us plates and cutlery. Out came the roasted chicken, steamed bread and Oros from the picnic basket. After our sumptuous dinner, Aunty checked outside the door where another train steward had put linen and blankets in a canvas duffel bag.

The linen was white and crisp. Aunty made up the beds. You could turn the reclining part of the couch into a bunk bed. After we washed in our basin, it was time to sleep. I slept in the top bunk, tucked neatly between blankets. The bunk had belts for securing whoever was sleeping on it to prevent them from falling.

Morning came and we were in Cape Town. Mom had sent my cousin Bheki Simelane to pick us up. I don't remember if I knew I had a sister Nandi at this stage. Nandi is my younger sister, who is three years younger than me, born on 27 June 1968. I just remember we got along very well when we met during this visit. She was roughly four years old at that point. I also remember that she was this scrawny girl who only spoke Afrikaans with our cousin Andile Simelane – Aunt Beryl Sisulu's son. Andile is Aunt Beryl's son with my Uncle Sion, who is my mother's elder brother. Aunt Beryl is my aunt twice, as she is also my father's cousin.

Back to Nandi. This scrawny sister of mine was a tomboy of note. While I liked playing house, Nandi loved playing marbles with the boys. During this visit, I was also introduced to my maternal grandmother, whom I called Ouma to differentiate between my grandmothers. I never really understood why Nandi stayed with Mom for longer than I ever did. Perhaps Mom wanted to have at least one of her children with her.

The defiance of apartheid laws runs in my family. You see, both Mom and Ouma lived in 7th Avenue, Retreat, in Cape Town. Retreat was an exclusively coloured area, according to the Group Areas Act. Ouma married a coloured man whose first name I do not remember. Upon getting married, she took his last name, De Jager, and so did my mother. Mom was known in Retreat by the name Molly de Jager, as to not be exposed, and Ouma was known as Lilian de Jager. Mom lived in a lavish *pondotjie*; a name given to a corrugated shack in Cape Town in those days. It had beautiful wallpaper. The *pondotjie* had three large rooms: a kitchen, living/dining room and a bedroom. I shared the sleeper couch with Aunt Maki during this visit. Nandi slept with Mom. There was also Uncle Phineas, who was a constant visitor. I liked him.

I enjoyed this visit and before long it was time to head back. Mom bought me a lot of clothes during the visit, the latest fashion. Among my new outfits was this red and white bell-bottom pair of trousers with a matching tank top, which I loved to bits. Because of these gifts, while growing up I was always on trend. After the holidays, I was back in Orlando and back at school.

In June 1972, we moved to Cofimvaba. Cofimvaba is a village town, 79 km from Queenstown, both in present-day Eastern Cape province. To a seven-year-old, this was another adventure. Rundu bought a shop from Mr Muller, the local retailer who was relocating to East London. She explained to us much, much later when I was in my teens that the sale was facilitated by Chief Kaiser Daliwonga Matanzima (also known as Chief K.D. Matanzima). The chief and Granddad come from the same lineage tree, the Royal House of the Thembus. Their great grandfather, King Ngubengcuka, my great-great grandfather, ruler of the Thembus from 1800–1830, is believed to have had five wives.

King Ngubengcuka, one of the greatest monarchs, who is credited with having united the Thembus, died in 1832. As was the custom, he had wives from the principal royal houses: Great House, from which the heir is selected; the Right-Hand House; and Ixhiba, a minor house which is referred to by some as the Left-Hand House. It is the task of the sons from Ixhiba, or the Left-Hand House, to settle royal disputes. Mtirara, the eldest son of the Great House, succeeded Ngubengcuka and his sons were Ngangelizwe and Matanzima. Sabata, who ruled the Thembus from 1954, was the grandson of Ngangelizwe, a senior to Kaiser Daliwonga. K.D. Matanzima was also the former chief minister of Transkei. Chief K.D. Matanzima was Granddad's nephew by law and by custom he was a descendant of Matanzima, the son of Ngubengcuka. The eldest son of the Ixhiba house was Simakade, whose younger brother was Mandela, Granddad's grandfather.

Therefore, when Rundu was looking for property three years after my father's death, she turned to Chief K.D. Matanzima, who by custom and tradition was obliged to assist, as she was his uncle's wife. It is also not by coincidence that she chose Cofimvaba of all the villages around the Transkei. Cofimvaba is intricately intertwined with the history of the Thembus. In 1830, the Great House under King Ngubengcuka continued to experience political instability, which resulted in the abrupt departure of Queen Nonesi, the widowed great wife of Ngubengcuka, and his two sons, Mtirara and Matanzima, from the Mgwali Great Place, which fell under the chieftainship of Joyi. About a decade later, in 1840, Mtirara, the eldest son of Ngubengcuka, was installed as the king of abaThembu. His great place was at Rhodana.

Around 1860, Ngangelizwe, the son of Mtirara, returned to Mgwali and was installed as King of abaThembu at Mgwali. Queen Nonesi remained in Gqebenya with Raxoti Matanzima, even after her son had returned to Mgwali. Shortly thereafter, the land around St Marks, the present-day Cofimvaba, was vacated by amaGcaleka, due to the Nongqawuse cattle-killing episode. In 1865, the colonial government offered this land to the residents of Lady Frere. This offer was accepted by four of the chiefs, namely Matanzima of amaHala, Ndarala of amaNdungwane, Gecelo of amaGcina and Stokwe of amaVundle. Queen Nonesi, however, refused to move from Lady Frere and was consequently banished to Libode by the colonial government.

What is important to note about this brief history is how the towns of Cofimvaba, Lady Frere and Libode were to play an important role in my life. Years later, after schooling in Cofimvaba, I was to train as a general nurse in Lady Frere and do my midwifery in Libode.

Chief Matanzima must have chosen Cofimvaba for Rundu, his uncle's wife, for its strategic business position and not only to offer her moral support from a close distance; he lived in Qamata, which was very close. Cofimvaba was the hub of business. All neighbouring villages did their shopping there.

Compared to a small yard in Orlando, the one in Cofimvaba was a massive seven to eight acres. There was a fowl run complete with indigenous chickens and leghorns. For the first time in my life I was eating fresh eggs that had just been laid. Rundu taught me how to collect the eggs from the coop. I saw chicks being hatched. She even taught me how to know if an egg was off without breaking it. I don't remember missing Orlando, only my next-door neighbours, twins Harry and Harold.

The layout of the main business district of Cofimvaba was as such: diagonally across Rundu's shop was Mrs Magaqa's shop. Next door to Mrs Magaqa was Theo Fitz's shop, which was bought by the Pambukas in the late '70s. Adjacent from us were the Mbesezas, who ran a filling station complete with a workshop. Then there was the local post office and opposite it was a shop owned by the Batalas. A church was located opposite the Batalas' shop, Methodist or Anglican, I can't remember exactly. Lastly, there was a shop which we called *emaGrikeni* because it was owned by a Greek family. At the end of Main Street was the Roman Catholic Church, which had a boarding school.

Cofimvaba had two major gravel-road streets: Main Street, where most of the shops were located, and High Street, which had other shops including two butcheries, a magistrate's court and a bakery.

We had two local doctors, Dr J.J. Mabaso and Dr M.M. Mpambani. Dr Mpambani was also the local surgeon.

There were two hotels in Comfimvaba, Down Hotel and Central Hotel. Down Hotel was opposite our house. From the veranda of our house we could see almost everything going on on the lawns of the hotel. This is where I first saw ZCC (Zion Christian Church) and its band in all its glory when Bishop Lekganyane came to town. I will never forget the melody of the band or the discipline of the congregants.

Cofimvaba was one of those village towns where everybody knew pretty much everybody. This can be annoying for teenagers, as I grew up in an era where every adult could discipline you if you were out of order or tell your parents and they'd deal with you.

I started school at Cofimvaba Village School in July 1972. The following years were a blur of making new friends, one of whom is still my friend to this day, Landiwe Menera.

In 1974, my sister, Nandi, and cousin Andile joined us in Cofimvaba. They were both to start Grade One that year. This tomboy sister of mine who did not speak a word of isiXhosa and preferred playing marbles over playing house, was to come live with us, and I took on the role of being big sister with zeal. In Cofimvaba, playing house meant stealing a bit of mealie meal to cook in cleaned-out empty canned-food containers, or cooking *unomgcana* – striped mice – which was deemed to stop bed wetting. This was the highlight of our holidays.

The first school we all attended together was at a Balfour homestead and it went up to Grade Four. My first teacher there was Mrs Mnqandi and her daughter, Singathwa, was in the same class as the one I was in. By the time I reached Grade Four, a new school was completed called Cofimvaba Junior Secondary School (Cofimvaba JSS).

It was at this new school that I developed my love for reading. We had a double reading period every week when you had to go to the school library, choose a book to read and you would be quizzed on it. This is where I got exposed to fairy tales like *Cinderella, Tom Thumb, Jack and the Beanstalk*, and so on. It was also here that I was first introduced to Brownies and Girl Guides. Sadly, I was forbidden to join them, as Rundu was a devout Jehovah's Witness. You see, it was forbidden for Jehovah's Witnesses to salute a flag, as was required for both Brownies and Girl Guides to receive their pins and emblems. This rule is referenced in Exodus 20, verses four and five, where it says, '*You must not make for yourself an idol of any kind or an image of anything in the heavens or earth or in the sea. You must not bow down to them or worship them, for I, the Lord your God, am a jealous God, who will not tolerate your affection for any other Gods.*' Bowing or saluting a flag constitutes worship for Jehovah's Witnesses.

I also learnt how to sew at Cofimvaba JSS. Mrs Mnqandi was our sewing teacher. She had moved to Cofimvaba JSS after the school was built. She would make you undo your top stitching if there was even a hint of untidiness. All manner of grooming for both boys and girls was taught at this school.

We had an English teacher called Ms Mthonjeni, *owayengakubetha uphambane* (who would give you the hiding of your life) if you made grammatical mistakes. On certain days, she would come into class and say, 'Against the wall'. We all knew what this meant. Ms Mthonjeni, on such days, was not playing games. Against the wall meant we were to leave our desks, with everything on them, and line up against the wall for a language tenses quiz. To this day, I am reminded of her when I hear a person making grammatical mistakes. Such was her teaching. Ms Mthonjeni also loved wearing heels and I loved watching her walk in them.

We also had Mr Mtyaphi, a brilliant maths teacher. In hindsight, it's a pity I took more to biology than maths. Mr Mtyaphi was so good at maths that when he was transferred to Mcumngco Secondary School to take on the role of principal, Rundu had me transferred there as well the following year. I was to do only Standard Seven at that school. I did not like it much. For starters, Mcumngco was far. It was a good hour's walk from home versus the seven to ten minutes it would take me to get to Cofimvaba. The floors were not plastered, which meant every Friday we had to apply cow dung to them to keep them neat. I had never done this before. Our group did this every alternate Friday. By the end of the year, in 1979, I was a pro in *ukusinda* – applying cow dung. I had to carry fresh cow dung from home – this was the easy part, as Rundu had cows. I would mix this with water, but not too much. The consistency mattered. My first attempt at *ukusinda* was so messy that I had to go back and sweep the residue after it had dried up.

Another thing I hated was that since we had to walk to school, my shoes would be full of dust by the time I reached the school and I had to shine them again. We also had to cross a river that had no bridge. It was dangerous during summer when it rained, as the banks of the river would swell. To cross this river, you had to pull your uniform up, take off your shoes and put your books on your head and cross. There were scary moments. All in all, going to school at Mcumngco Secondary was quite an experience.

Around the time I turned 14, we were joined by my cousin Mandla, who was four years old. Mandla is my first cousin and the firstborn of Uncle Makgatho and Réne Mosehle. Rundu wanted all her grandchildren to be groomed by her. Mandla was this very chubby light-skinned child who loved food. Rundu had taught me to bake by this time and I had taken to cooking and baking with zeal. To this day, I still love cooking. One day, during school holidays, I felt like baking a sponge cake. Since Rundu had the shop I did not have to buy my ingredients. All I had to do was write the list of what I needed, go to the store and ask any of Rundu's older cousins who were working at the shop to give me all the ingredients. But they had to make sure everything was written in the credit book for household stuff so Rundu could keep track of how much she had to pay the shop at the end of the month.

Now that I had the ingredients, Rama, self-raising flour, milk, sugar and vanilla essence, I set them on a tray on the kitchen table. I stepped out of the kitchen to get eggs from the chicken coop, and I was ready to start. I loved to first cream the margarine and gradually add sugar to make a smooth, creamy batter. I looked for the Rama. '*Rama, wawuphi?*' (Rama, where are you?). I even thought I had forgotten to get it, and then I heard a noise from under the table. It was Mandla eating the Rama. Imagine that! He'd eaten a quarter of the 250g block of margarine.

There was one thing Nandi and Mandla had in common, which was crying incessantly, but Mandla paled in comparison to Nandi. Nandi could howl – I say howl, as there would be no tears – for two hours straight. If you gave her a hiding close to the evening, you'd regret it, as she'd howl in a monotonous voice sitting next to the stove for days. One day, one of our aunts who'd just had enough of this crying pulled a trick on her. It was raining and we could not play outside. Nandi was driving everyone nuts with her crying. As she was crying, my aunt came close to her and called me to come and see. She was pointing to the hollow part at the base of her neck where the clavicle meets the sternum. When one cries, this part indents naturally, but as she was pointing to Nandi's one, she pretended this was abnormal. She said, 'I think this child is going to die soon. The more she cries the more this indent grows deeper and deeper. Soon it will go so deep she won't be able to breathe anymore, and she'll die.' I played along. That stopped her dead in her tracks. Rundu was in Queenstown, so there was no one Nandi could verify this with. As soon as Rundu came home, Nandi ran to her. Rundu, of course being tired, just told her there was no such thing. That day marked the end of the incessant monotonous cry because Nandi was not sure who to believe.

From an early age, I learnt that laziness does not pay. One of the chores I had as the eldest grandchild was to start the fire in our coal stove. One afternoon we were playing uBati, a game played with a tennis ball. The game was intense, and it was about to be my turn when my aunt called me to come start the fire. I was annoyed and decided to take a short cut on my usual method. To make a fire that will take, you must first put wood and kindle, set them alight and wait a few minutes for the fire to strengthen before you add the coal. On this day, I had no patience. As soon as there was a big flame, I added the coal, closed the front latch and went off to continue with our game. Of course, the fire died out. I was called again to fix up my mess. At this point, I was livid because I knew I would have to take the coal out, get fresh wood and start the fire again. I was having none of that. In the corner cupboard next to the stove there was always a gallon of kerosene. I poured some in a bottle and headed for the stove. No one was paying attention to all of this. My aim was to pour most of the kerosene on top of the coal. I would then light a piece of paper and light the fire from the ash grid below. I had done this several times before with resonably good results. I poured the kerosene, with my face right in front of the stove and my hand inside the stove, not knowing that there were still embers at the bottom that were burning. All I remember was this backdraft of fire coming out the front of the stove. I will never tell you how I got out of that kitchen. I ran like a mad person. My hand felt as if it was on fire. I ran to the outside tap to run cold water over my hand. Every time I took my hand out of the water it would burn again. I repeated this process for close to 30 minutes. The next day I just had minor blisters on my knuckles, but my hairline, above my forehead, was singed, and I had no eyelashes, as they were burnt too. Never again did I take shortcuts when making the fire. It would be years later, when I was training as a nurse, that I would learn the first aid for burns is to apply cold water.

Growing up in a village was really what taught me to enjoy the simple things in life. Deep down, I'm still a simple girl with the naiveté of my village life. When you grow up in such an environment, you learn to trust people easily and you develop a certain value system. This is a value system of giving, of *Ubuntu*. Village people, back when I was growing up, had a sense of sharing with their neighbours if they were in need. I guess this is why I ended up in social activism; it's because of how I was raised.

While I enjoyed Cofimvaba immensely, I also enjoyed visiting my mom in Cape Town. The first year Nandi came to join me in Cofimvaba, Uncle Phineas came to fetch us. At the time, I did not know he was my stepfather. Although I had met and seen him in my mother's house in Cape Town, it did not occur to me that he was my stepfather. Nandi had referred to him as Daddy many a time and each time I corrected her that our father had died, and his name was Thembekile. In my 10-year-old mind, I felt she should have known this. I could not comprehend how it was that I knew who my father was, and Nandi did not, but she was just over 13 months old when he died. I was determined to set the record straight when we got to Cape Town.

When Uncle Phineas arrived to get us, I was very excited, as this would be the first time I would travel by car to Cape Town. We took the Garden Route through Port Elizabeth and Knysna. Throughout the journey I was calling our 'dad' Uncle Phineas and he would correct me every time. I was quite resolute I would call him Dad only once I had confirmed with my mom.

We reached Cape Town and when Uncle Phineas did not leave the house that night, I decided to ask Mom about the issue. I can't remember exactly how I asked. All I remember is that Mom brought out two albums with their wedding pictures. I did not receive the news well but hid it. It's amazing how my almost 11-year-old psyche had learnt how to hide pain, disappointment and anger. Yes, anger. I felt that I was old enough for Mom to tell me she was getting remarried. Nandi did not remember or know my father; I did. She owed me the truth. This anger towards Mom would resurface when I fell pregnant with my firstborn, Tembela.

I soon forgot about this ordeal, or buried it in my subconscious, and enjoyed the holidays. Cape Town was such fun.

Every December holiday we spent in Cape Town, we went to Mnandi Beach with Aunty Tofe (Mom's cousin), her husband Uncle Kenneth Sanders and their children, my cousins Jennifer, Kenneth Jr, Esther and Dora. Our parents would pack sumptuous goods in picnic baskets, and we'd spend the whole of Christmas Day on the beach. We wore our brand-new Christmas clothes complete with white bobby socks that had lace at the top. Our houses would be decorated with Christmas lights. New Year's Day would be spent in Platboom Beach, which I loved more than Mnandi Beach, as it was quite a distance from Retreat. We would drive in convoy. I loved Mom's Tempest convertible. It was red and white. I think it is why to this day I love sports cars. Platboom would be a blast, as we could swim. The ocean was not as rocky as Mnandi Beach was, at least where black people could swim. Even the ocean was segregated.

That year I asked for a bicycle from Phineas – Dad as I now called him. The holidays came to an end, and we went back to Cofimvaba.

The following year, Dad came to fetch us and this time we drove through the Karoo, Graaff-Reinet, Cradock and De Aar. That year I was introduced to the Queen of Soul, Aretha Franklin. We listened to audio tapes of Aretha's music all the way to Cape Town. These audio tapes were not TDK or Sony. They were the bulky type before the slim version was invented.

Rundu told me years later that the second time Dad came

to fetch us, it was also to ask her if he could legally adopt us. Rundu refused.

The next time we went to Cape Town, we flew. It was 1978 and it was my first flight as an unaccompanied minor. My first flight ever had been when we flew to Cape Town with Rundu to collect Dad's remains in 1969. Although I was only four years old at the time, I remember the incident vividly. I was wearing a coat, thick toddler stockings and a hat. The clear picture in my head is that of Ouma, holding me by the hand as we stand outside the airport building, presumably waiting for Dad's coffin to be offloaded from the plane. I can't remember if this was Cape Town or Johannesburg airport, but if I was to take an educated guess, I would say it was Johannesburg. Mom is not visible in this memory, but both my grandmothers are.

I was 13 and Nandi 10. Rundu drove us to Ben Schoeman Airport, now renamed East London Airport. We were given tags with 'unaccompanied minor' written on them and had to wait for all the other passengers to board before we did with a flight attendant. Nandi would narrate on my 50th birthday how I made her feel safe by holding her hand and reassuring her. I do not remember doing that. I guess I thought instinctively that she must have been nervous. For me it was another adventure.

Back and forth we went every December holiday, that is, until I fell pregnant with Tembela.

Chapter 2

Boarding school

As the saying goes, 'Time flies when you're having fun.' Before I knew it, I was a teenager and because the local schools only went up to Standard Seven, I had to leave home to attend boarding school.

I was 15 years old when I started boarding school at Nyanga High School in 1980. Nyanga High School is just outside Engcobo, along the road to Umtata. It was one of the schools built shortly after the apartheid government formed the Bantustan states within South Africa, with the Eastern Cape becoming the Transkei. Apartheid laws created these artificial borders and suddenly we had to carry travel documents to travel between Cofimvaba, which was now in Transkei, while Queenstown was in South Africa.

Anyway, Nyanga was a brand-new high-rise boarding school built after Transkei 'gained independence' in 1976. It had four floors, immaculate dormitories, showers and ablution facilities. I loved my days at Nyanga. I was in Standard 8F and home economics was one of our subjects. I took to this subject like you cannot believe. I became a pro at baking Swiss rolls from scratch. To this day, Nandi tells my children, no one bakes Swiss rolls like I do (toot-toot!).

If Cofimvaba JSS introduced me to the love of reading, Nyanga introduced me to movies. Even now, I can spend an entire weekend at home binge-watching movies. I particularly loved Western movies. Almost every Saturday at Nyanga we had movies in the dining hall. It was also a chance for me and Thoza, my very first boyfriend, to snuggle together at the back of the hall, watching whatever movie was showing.

I always tell my close friends that if there's ever a time parents lose influence over their children, it is when they send them to boarding school. At boarding school, you must make your own decisions without parental guidance and yet you are not a fully fledged adult. As much as teens are considered unruly, it is this period that can build character. This, to me, was a time when the value system that was instilled in me would be tested.

My relationship with Thoza proved that it was then that Rundu lost her parental guidance and influence over me. I was still a virgin. Girls would talk about their sexual experience and I had nothing to tell. I felt very embarrassed by this, as it meant I was backward. I came from a Jehovah's Witness household where boyfriends and pre-marital sex was forbidden.

Ours was a relationship of puppy love of just kissing and fondling. It's a little hard to come from an extremely strict and sheltered life and be thrown in the deep end of having to understand this flurry of emotions and feelings that you've never even heard anyone talk about in your own home or among the friends you grew up with. I had to figure things out on my own. Funnily enough, it was a woman who taught me how to figure out my own body.

At high school we had this Big Sister or 'Mommy' system, where if an older student liked you, you became her baby. My 'mommy' came from one of the affluent families in All Saints. You can imagine how she spoilt me. Some nights we would share a bed. One night when we were sharing a bed she started kissing me and touching me and, I must admit, my 15-year-old body that was raging with hormones liked it. Suddenly I felt my body heating up like a volcano. I experienced such ecstasy, it felt as if I was floating. This experience scared the living daylights out of me and I avoided sharing a bed with her after that. Fortunately, it happened towards the end of the year and the following year I did not return to Nyanga. It would be years later that I would understand what happened to me that night. I had no one to talk to about it. This is one of the reasons I never sent my children to boarding school – the lack of guidance and feelings of being lost. Yet I would never trade any of the years at boarding school for anything, for I believe they plant the seed of self-sufficiency.

Thoza was from Queenstown and politically active. As Jehovah's Witnesses are also apolitical, I knew nothing about politics save for the stories we read from *Watchtower* magazines about the persecution of fellowship brothers who were imprisoned for refusing to salute the flag, like in Germany and Russia, or refusing to join the army. Thoza awakened a sleeping giant in me – that of defiance. He would tell me of the inequities that existed in Queenstown between the township and the suburbs. He taught me a lot about myself.

Two weeks before schools closed for the December vacation, we embarked on a strike. Having been conscientised by Thoza, I was actively involved. The food we were eating did not match the school fees we were paying, and we were protesting for better food. As it usually happens, there's always someone who is a snitch and will sing like a canary and rat everybody out. All who partook in the strike were called one by one to the matron's office. The deal was if you could rat on the ringleaders, you would not be punished or expelled from the school.

My turn came. I can still see that scene in my mind's eye – the matron and boarding master interrogating me. Of course, since Thoza was one of the ringleaders I could not rat him out. I received 10 floggings on my back with a shambok plus a no-return remark on my report card. These floggings cut my back very badly and I had to return home with wounds. During those days, a school report was posted home and took up to three weeks to arrive there. Rundu had a habit of wanting to wash all of us when we returned from boarding school, as she said we had '*ntsente*' or a build-up of dirt. This '*ntsente*' would be removed using a pumice stone and would flake off like '*umphokoqo*'(pap with fluffy consistency). This time was no different. Rundu asked me to run a bath the day I returned. As she came into the bathroom and asked me to undress and get into the bath, two things scared me the most: that she would discover the still-raw welts on my back – Jehovah's Witnesses we were forbidden to partake in any strike or protest action – and I would have to tell her about being expelled from Nyanga.

As it turned out, I did not have to worry about any of that. The minute she saw those welts she went ballistic. No one could give us a hiding but her. If the schools were still open, she would have gone to tell the matron herself to never touch me again. The expulsion was not even necessary, as she told me I was not returning to a school where the matron was so sadistic. You do not understand the sense of relief I felt.

The following year I started school at Daliwonga High

School. Although Daliwonga was closer to home, being about 10 km away, it was a culture shock for me. Where at Nyanga we had single beds, at Daliwonga we had bunk beds. I had to look after Nandi as well, as she joined me at the school. Each dormitory had four cubicles, each cubicle had four bunk beds and we had to share the beds. There would be eight students in a cubicle and 32 pupils in a dormitory, versus 16 pupils in a dormitory at Nyanga. There were two blocks of dormitories for girls, built in a split-level, upper and lower block. The upper block was for juniors, who were packed like sardines, and the lower block was for senior students, who were less packed than us and who had no bunk beds.

The beds were made from *ikayo* – straw. There were bed bugs all over the walls and only two bathrooms to be shared among almost 300 girl students. I do not have to tell you what a nightmare it was to bathe in the morning. First wake-up bell went off at 4 am and if you wanted to bathe in peace and with hot water, you had to wake up then. If you went to bathe at around 5 am, the bathrooms would be gridlocked, literally.

Picture this: there are only eight sinks and six shower cubicles. If you enter the bathroom at its peak time all you can see are naked bodies against naked bodies, jostling for hot water, some splashing water on themselves to rinse off soap. You run out and dry yourself in your dormitory because the bathroom is too packed for you to dry yourself properly.

At 6:45 am, the first bell rings for all to go to breakfast. The second bell rings at 7 am and you must exit and stand in front of the hostel according to your grade class and then in single file enter the dining hall. If you are late you get cited by a prefect.

It's clear to see that I hated Daliwonga. The only positive thing was that Rundu was close by and I could ask for anything that Nandi and I needed. It would not take long for her to come by to drop it off. We had to meet with Rundu three times a week. The food was horrendous. Food would be dished in big aluminium dishes with just a few pieces of meat on top of this huge mound of *umngqusho* (samp and beans). We would sit 10 per table and a prefect was dispatched to each table to cite anyone seen talking. I mean … I found it ridiculous that we were expected to eat in silence, and this resulted in many citations. After a certain number of citations, you received punishment – either cleaning the bathrooms on weekends or scrubbing the dining hall. It was at Daliwonga that my non-conformity reared its ugly head.

Daliwonga was predominantly Methodist. Morning and evening service were compulsory. I did not mind these services, but I hated the SCM (Student Christian Movement), led by Ms Martins. You must remember that my Christian grounding was that of Jehovah's Witnesses. The notion that after the pastor preached, you had to be seized with Holy Ghost's power and go in front of the congregation to say they were saved was ridiculous to me. My 'refusal' to be saved earned me Ms Martins's wrath and extreme dislike. I really did not care about this.

At Daliwonga, it was difficult to skip church unless you were ill. The prefects and Ms MaWindow (our matron) would search through the hostel with a fine-tooth comb. We gave our matron this nickname because her office, which was at the front of the hostel facing the carpark and dining hall, had huge windows where she could see the comings and goings of just about anyone. She was always glued to that window, hence the name.

Students always found a way of beating the system, and I was no different. A couple of Sundays, I managed to dodge the church service. Onke and a few of our friends figured it out. She was a very close friend of mine who came from East

London. She arrived at Daliwonga a year after I arrived. We were allocated the same dormitory and were also in the same class. My physical education teacher, Mr Amuah, liked both Onke and me. He would ask us to wash his car, which was a beautiful Mercedes. Our reward was Kentucky, and he would buy it for us whenever he went to Queenstown. Chief K.D. Matanzima, who was president at that time, saw fit to bring teachers and doctors from Ghana, Kenya and Uganda to come to the Transkei. Mr Amuah was one of these teachers. He would years later become my uncle by marrying Aunt Maki.

Early in the year, around January or February, was when the schools' inter-house athletic games were held. Our athletics teacher made me hate athletics. We were all forced to wake up at 4 am and jog. Not that I couldn't jog or run. I just did not see the need to do this at the crack of dawn. I have never been a morning person. I don't understand people that are so chirpy in the morning.

Although I was fast in the 100m and 200m races, when the inter-school athletics games were held, we discovered that the girls from Mahlubini were faster. The gap between us and them was so large, it was as if we were chilling and not even competing. Most schools hated athletes from Mahlubini, as they were the fastest in our district.

Like Nyanga, Daliwonga was a co-ed school, but unlike Nyanga, boys would climb over the walls at night to have sex with their girlfriends. This was mortifying, as there was no privacy. The setup was such that if the person you were sharing a bunk bed with had their boyfriend visiting that night, they would ask you to find an alternative sleeping place. This practice ended one night when one of the athletics teachers who stayed at the hostel was going to her room very late. The boys would come after 10:30 pm when the lights had been switched off. The boys' hostel was built similarly to that of the girls, so they knew their way around. This teacher had been marking papers. As she was walking past, she saw the boys scurrying into the girls' dorms. She screamed: '*Nanga amakhwenkwe eMzana!*' (The boys are in the girls' hostel!) All hell broke loose. The lights were switched back on. The boys scurried around and ran out of Mzana, the girls' dorm. By Monday there was razor wire on top of the walls of Mzana, and this ended the pastime.

By the time I was in Grade 12 I had a new boyfriend. Thoza, after being expelled like I was from Nyanga, went into exile. The last thing I heard about his whereabouts was that he had gone missing. My new boyfriend, Sbongile, was a talented football player who I was not allowed to be close to at school. As I mentioned, at Daliwonga, my non-conformity flourished. During a soccer match, I broke this rule. I felt like if they did not want us to talk to boys, they should've had a girls-only school and not a co-ed. As my luck would have it, we were discovered by Ms Martins. We were reported to the principal, Mr Greef, a very strict German man who used to wear brightly coloured suits ... I mean who wears purple or red suits?

Ms Martins was of course very jubilant as she said she'd long predicted that I would amount to nothing. And this somehow proved it. The cheek of this woman. Who had died and made her God? By Monday we were both suspended and asked to come to the school with our parents. At least I did not have far to go, as Cofimvaba was about 10 km from Daliwonga. Sbongile lived in Engcobo and would have to catch a bus to get home. Engcobo is 63 km away from Cofimvaba. The way we walked back to Cofimvaba was so comical. We'd walk together but were on the lookout for any dust signalling an oncoming car; the roads were made of gravel, you see. The car could belong to any of our teachers. When we saw this dust, Sbongile would run to the opposite side of the road until the car was far enough way for the driver not to see us. He would then come back to walk on my side of the road.

I wished this walk would last forever, as I was too scared to tell Rundu why I had been suspended. When I got home, I learnt that she was in Queenstown to buy stock for the shop. My heart was in my mouth when she arrived. After hearing my story, she was so annoyed. She said, '*Hamb'uyokha uswazi.*' (Go and get a switch). This switch would be from a peach tree outside. This method of punishment baffled me as an adult. Your parent, who is angry with you, asks you to go and choose the weapon you will be punished with. This is a comedy of comedies. Of course, I got the lightest switch. I already knew my strategy. Rundu rarely hit us and she was a sucker for tears. After three or four switches on my legs, I started wailing and she stopped.

The next day we both drove back to school and she asked that I be pardoned, as I would not repeat this offence. I did, very discreetly though. Ms Martins and our principal made the cardinal mistake of professing that they both felt I would amount to nothing. Rundu almost chopped their heads off. Sadly, a close relative repeated those words to me in 2012 when I had not lived up to her expectations. I applied the same attitude I did back then: no one has the right to condemn you because even God does not condemn anyone.

Before I knew it, my time at Daliwonga was over, but since my Matric results were not good. Granddad insisted that I repeat Matric. I had got to know him through the letters he had begun writing to me from when I was 10 years old – all from prison. Because of my non-conformist attitude, I was not allowed back at Daliwonga. Rundu had to look for a school elsewhere. She asked one of the

Jehovah's Witness brothers, Brother Majeke, to assist her. Ngangelizwe High School, in the township of Ngangelizwe, just outside Mthalha, was one of the best schools in 1983, with the best Matric results. By the time we went there, admissions were closed, and the school was full. But I was granted admission at Nozuko High School, which was a second branch of Ngangelizwe.

That year, I stayed with the Majekes in Ngangelizwe. I hated it. Every fortnight I would catch a bus and go home to Cofimvaba. At the end of that year, I got a good pass, a Matric exemption, but my maths result was still not very good. I wanted to study medicine at the University of Cape Town, and the requirements were a good result in maths and science.

The following year, in 1984, I was admitted at Clarkebury Teacher Training College. Clarkebury is a mission school built on the land donated to the Methodist Church by my great-great grandfather, King Ngubengcuka, in the 1800s to build a school and a church.

If I thought Daliwonga's hostel was terrible, nothing prepared me for Clarkebury. This school had no proper bathrooms. Bathrooms consisted of four walls, with no proper door and falling corrugated aluminium coverings. We had to wash in buckets with cold water. The toilets were a health hazard of epic proportions. Never had I seen pit latrines with maggots before.

The kitchen was so archaic it was not funny. I saw, for the first time in my life, rudimentary pots. Big pots attached to the wall, at the bottom of which there was an opening, like a small stove, where you made the fire to cook. If the fire was too high, there was no way of removing the pot from the fire, as it was attached to the wall, which meant the food at the bottom of the pot was always burnt.

At Clarkebury I saw for the first time a person who was demon possessed, *amafufunyana* as we called them. She was in our dormitory. The attack came at night. This girl was in some form of a trance and was speaking in a deep male voice that she did not have ordinarily. She was writhing on the floor as our chaplain prayed over her. There was what I believed a myth then that if you came too close, when the demons were cast out successfully, they would seek another person to possess. I have to say, I watched the attack and exorcism only once, out of curiosity. It was such a scary experience.

After the mid-year break, I did not return to Clarkebury, as I discovered I was pregnant. I had been seeing Tembela's father from the middle of my second Matric year, when I was a pupil at Nozuko High School.

After Tembela's birth, I chose to not return to the college. I told Rundu, in fact I threatened, that she couldn't drag me back to Clarkebury with a dozen horses.

When Tembela was five months old, I started my training as a general nurse. I loved every minute of my training. Our group was called 5/85, which referred to a group intake of May 1985.

Chapter 3

Family

I HAVE A LARGE FAMILY. I GREW up with cousins, aunts and uncles, from both my maternal and paternal sides. Rundu was the youngest in her family and had three siblings – Kalep, Simon and Kate.

To the best of my knowledge, Kalep's children were Nomakhaya, Nomaledi, Daluxolo and Thembeka, all bearing the last name of Mase. There were other children, but these were the ones who at one time or the other came to live with us in Cofimvaba. There was also Tozama Mase, although I'm not sure whose child she was. Aunts Nomakhaya, Nomaledi and Thembeka all came to live with us in Cofimvaba and Rundu gave them jobs at her shop when they had their children.

Simon had the following children: Mongezi, Nzuzo, Nomaza, Nkululeko and Mluleki, all bearing the Mase last name. Grandpa Simon, or Khokho as we all called him, and Rundu were very close and when we relocated to Cofimvaba, we visited him a lot. Although most of Khokho's children did not come to live with us, I remember Uncle Mongezi from Orlando, with his wife, Aunt Elizabeth. Uncle Nkululeko did come to live with us in Cofimvaba, briefly.

Granny Kate, who had married a Mgudlwa, had nine children: Lulama (who partnered with Rundu to buy the shop in Cofimvaba), Nosisi, twins Cheeky and Victor, Mbulelo, Nomkoko and Maphelo. The other two died in infancy. Of Granny Kate's children – it was Aunt Lulama, or Aunty Peto (derived from Patricia), and her children who stayed with us. In fact, she and her children had preceded Rundu and me in the move to Cofimvaba. Her husband, Mr Motlakeng, had died a year or two after Dad died, leaving her with four children, Mphala, Emma, Mothusi and Tshidi. If my memory serves me correctly, her husband died in a car accident.

When we arrived in Cofimvaba, it was a full house. After about two years of Rundu and Aunty Lulama running the shop, they had a fall out, I don't know over what, and Rundu bought her out. It was shortly after that that we were joined by Rundu's nieces, aunts Nomakhaya, Nomaledi and Thembeka. I guess since Maliyavuza was a very big general dealer store, which was what it was renamed as when Rundu brought it, Rundu needed help and what better way for her to do that than to give her nieces employment.

In Cofimvaba I had cousins from my father's siblings. Rundu had three children. Dad gave her two grandchildren, Nandi and me. From Uncle Kgatho she got four grandchildren, all boys, Mandla, Ndaba, Mbuso and Andile, and Aunt Maki gave her three grandchildren, Tukwini, Dumani and Kwekwu and a stepdaughter, Adjoa. It was Uncle Kgatho and Aunt Maki's children that I grew up with. From Uncle Kgatho, Mandla and Ndaba stayed with us and from Aunt Maki, Tukwini and Dumani.

I also had two aunts who were my father's half-sisters,

Family

Aunt Zeni and Aunt Zindzi, only the term half-sister does not exist in African languages. It would be years before I could get acquainted with them and their children, my cousins.

You may ask where and how we lived with so many people. Rundu was really blessed with a vast property and had built extra rooms for all the children to live in. This is where I learnt to hold my own in any situation. We teased each other a lot. I had to develop a thick skin not to get upset.

What fun we had.

There was never a dull moment in Cofimvaba. We made our own skipping rope from *umsingizane*. We played hide and seek and board games from draughts to snakes and ladders. We played hopscotch too.

My life was very diverse from an early age. In Cofimvaba we had a strict upbringing in a conservative home, owing to Rundu, who lived and practised the Jehovah's Witness tenants to a tee. Then there was my life in Cape Town when we would visit Mom. Cape Town was such a contrast to Cofimvaba, as I could celebrate Christmas and go to the movies to watch a double feature with my other cousins from my maternal side. Basically, the rules were much more lax.

In Cape Town I got a chance to spend time and interact with my mother's side of the family. Mom was the youngest of Ouma's three children. Ouma's other children were sons, – Mgayeni, but we called him Uncle Shorty, and Uncle Sion. I never asked why Uncle Shorty was called thus, suffice to say I thought it was because he was short. Uncle Shorty lived mostly in Johannesburg, in Mofolo, Soweto, and was married to Aunt Matlakala. Uncle Shorty had eight children: Party, Butikisi, Bongani, Veli, Raymond, Nomaswazi, Nompi and Queen. Since Nomaswazi stayed with Ouma, I spent a lot of time with her during all my visits to Cape Town.

Uncle Sion married my aunt Beryl Sisulu (my father's cousin) and thus she is my aunt twice, first by our blood relations (the Mases and Sisulus are cousins) and by marriage. Uncle Sion married Aunt Beryl after his first wife, Aunt Irene Simelane, died with Dad in the car accident. She was sitting in the passenger seat behind Dad. Uncle Sion had eight children too: Bheki, Themba, Andile, Zinhle, Zama, Thembi, Thulani and Pam. When Nandi came to join me in Cofimvaba, Andile came along too and lived with us for two years.

When Mom and Phineas finished building their house in Durban in 1981, in a township called Claremont, just outside Pinetown, Nandi and I were introduced to our stepsiblings. This was my first experience with stepsiblings. I remember growing up and asking myself how Mom could handle it. There was my sister Shirley and her brother Zola, whose mother lived in Gugulethu, in Cape Town, and we would see her whenever we went with Daddy Phineas to drop them off after they had come to visit in Retreat. Initially, I only knew the two of them before the house in Durban was built. When the house was completed, we were introduced to more stepsiblings. There was Gay, whose mother hailed from Cape Town too; Sifiso, whose mother was from KwaZulu-Natal; and Nomathemba.

The Durban house was a lavish house, built on a split level with three bedrooms and a modern kitchen with an eye-level Defy stove and a hob. This was all new to me, as in Cofimvaba we still used a coal stove and in Cape Town we used a gas stove.

Daddy Phineas was a generous man who loved all of us. He was proud of all of us. When we would spend the December holidays in Claremont and he was entertaining his friends, he would call us to come and recite poems in front of his friends to show us off. I must confess though that this used to annoy me at times, as it would sometimes be very late, and I just wanted to sleep.

As much as we lived in what is now called a blended family, it did at times irk me that I had to share a bedroom with so many of my stepsiblings. I was irritated even more so because as a young adult I hated sharing clothes, and our dad Phineas encouraged most of us girls who were more or less the same age and size, especially Shirley and me, to share our clothes. I soon learnt to adjust.

Having stepsiblings was not really a big issue, mainly because I spent most of my time with Rundu in Cofimvaba. In retrospect, I think this was the time the relationship with my mother became a little more distant. I could not understand why she had, in my view, not chosen my sister and me, and had instead chosen a life of having to bring up children that were not her own.

Growing up in this family, although it had its own set of challenges, taught me how to carve my own identity from an early age.

Part Two

Chapter 4

My father

I HAVE VERY FEW MEMORIES OF DAD. My sister Nandi has none, as he died when she was 13 months old.

Among my memories there are three vivid ones that stand out. The first is of when he bought me a cowboy outfit. I must have been about three years old or so. Our home in Orlando East had two pillars that held our gate in the front yard. Dad had dressed me in the cowboy outfit, complete with a cowboy hat, bell-bottom jeans and a gun holster. He was so proud of me. From time to time I would take this toy gun and play around with it and Dad would say, 'That's my girl.'

The second memory is of when he bought me a tricycle. At one end of Mashane Street there is a long road, built at something of an incline, that separates Orlando East and Diepkloof. He took me to this road to try and teach me how to ride my tricycle. Unfortunately, I fell off it, sustaining a long gash over my knee. To this day, I still have a scar from that fall.

The last memory is a painful one; it is the day of his

funeral. All I remember is that Dad lay in a coffin in Rundu's bedroom in Orlando. Mom, Ouma and just about everyone was wearing black. It was morning and people kept coming in to view him. Mom lifted me up and I saw that he had a veil over his face, which I tried to remove. I asked Mom why he looked so dark, as Dad was light skinned. Nowadays he would be called a yellow bone. There was a marquee in our front yard where the funeral service was conducted. Later on, Mom, Rundu, Ouma and I were in the hearse on our way to the cemetery and Mom was crying. Rundu kept telling her not to cry, as she would upset me. I cannot for the life of me remember where my sister was. It's only in pictures that I know she was around, as there is a picture of Ouma holding baby Nandi at Jan Smuts Airport, waiting for Dad's remains, along with Rundu and Aunt Maki. Everything after the funeral is a blur. Come to think of it, I never asked after my father following his funeral.

Did my four-year-old mind know what death was? How final it was and that you would never see the person again? Did somebody explain these things to me?

I really have no clue.

I have tried to find out from various people what my father was like as a young man. I get bits and pieces about him ranging from being a responsible person to being a trendy dresser. Uncle Matoto Zibi, who was his best friend at St Christopher's in Swaziland, describes him as a quiet person who was very loving. Mom would tell me the same except that he had a moody side to him.

To get to know him better and to get closer to Granddad, I would often ask Granddad about my dad after he was released from prison. It's important to note that I had to abandon that quest, as it became clear that Granddad did not want to speak about him. Whenever I asked him about

My father

Dad, it did not matter how happy and easy our conversation with him was, he would totally shut down and his face would be marred by a stony expression, with a faraway look in his eyes. I finally made peace with the fact that it was something he never wanted to speak about until Sahm Venter from the Nelson Mandela Foundation gave me copies of letters that Granddad wrote to various people around the time of Dad's death. It was then that I understood the depth of Grandad's pain and finally who he was: a kind young man.

In a letter Granddad wrote to Chief Mangosuthu Buthelezi dated 3 August 1969, he says the following about Dad:

The news was broken to me about 2:30 pm. Suddenly, my heart seemed to have stopped beating and the warmth that had freely flown in my veins for the last 51 years, froze into ice. For some time, I could neither think nor talk and my strength appeared to be draining out. Eventually, I found my way back to my cell with a heavy load on my shoulders and the last place a man stricken with sorrow should be.

To Rundu, on 16 July 1969:

Dear Evelyn

This afternoon the commanding officer informed me of a telegram received from attorney Mendel Leven of Johannesburg in which he reported the death of Thembi in a car accident in Cape Town on July 13.

I write to give you, Kgatho and Maki my deepest sympathy. I know more than anybody else living today just how devastating this cruel blow must have been to you for Thembi was your firstborn and the second child you have lost. I am also fully conscious of the passionate love you have for him and the efforts you made to train and prepare him to play his part in a complex industrial society. I am also fully aware of how Kgatho and Maki adored and respected him, the holidays and the good times they spent with him in Cape Town. In her letter written October 1967, Maki told me that Thembi helped you in buying all they needed. My late ma gave me details of the warm hospitality she received from him when she visited the island. Throughout the last five years up to March this year, Nobandla gave me interesting accounts of his attachment and devotion to the family and the personal interest he took in all his relatives. I last saw him five years ago during the Rivonia trial and always looked forward to these accounts for they were the main channel through which I was able to hear something of him.

The blow has been equally grievous to me. In addition to the fact that I had not seen him for at least 60 months, I was neither privileged to give him a wedding ceremony nor lay him to rest when that fatal hour had stuck. In 1967, I wrote him a long letter, drawing his attention to some matters which I thought were in his interest to attend to without delay. I looked forward to further correspondence and to meeting him and his family when I returned. All these expectations have now been taken away at the age of 24 and we will never see him again.

We shall be consoled and comforted by the fact that he had many good friends who join us in mourning his passing away. He fulfilled his duties to us as parents and has left us with an inheritance for which every parent is proud – a Molokazana and two lovely babies.

> *Once more I extend to you, Kgatho, Maki, my sincere condolences and that you will muster enough strength and courage to survive such a painful tragedy.*
>
> *Yours very sincerely*
> *Nelson*

What strikes me most about this letter is that even as early as 1967 Granddad had an unwavering belief and conviction that he would be released.

My father had felt very lost when Granddad was imprisoned. In a letter Granddad wrote to Mama Winnie the same day he had written to Rundu, he talks about Dad wearing his clothes. He also noted the strain that Dad took when he thought Granddad would get the death penalty. In the same letter Granddad writes:

> *During the Rivonia case he sat behind me one day. I kept looking back, nodding to him and giving him a broad smile. At the time it was generally believed that we would certainly be given the extreme penalty, and this was clearly written across his face. Though he nodded back as many times as I did to him, not once did he return the smile.*

These letters that Granddad wrote to various people around Dad's death give me a glimpse of the type of person Dad was.

In another letter Granddad wrote to Uncle Kgatho, dated 28 July 1969, he describes dad as 'a shield that protected you against danger and that helped you build your self-confidence and courage'.

In the same letter he goes on to say:

In Cape Town he provided a home for you where you could happily spend extra long holidays, meet new friends and learn about your country and people.

I think it fit and proper to highlight but one striking virtue of his which strikes a deep impression on me. His love and devotion to you, Maki, Zeni and Zindzi and relatives, generally created the image of a man who respected family ties and who was destined to play an important role in the upbringing, education and developing of his children and sisters. He had become the object of love, education and respect and a source of pride to the family.

Oh! How I have wished over the years to have had him around until I had my own children. I have often wondered how our lives as his daughters would have been had he not died at such a young age.

As I read these letters, I was beginning to put together the pieces of this puzzle called Dad. Granddad poured out his pain in these letters as a form of healing.

1 August 1970, a year after Dad died, he writes the following to Zuki. She is Granddad's niece from his eldest sister, Baliwe.

Our dear Zuki

The death of Thembi was a bitter blow to me for he was an intimate friend. The relationship of father and son was but the foundation stone upon which we were building more intimate connections and it really hurt me to know that I would never see him again.

There was a time during the last eight years when nothing could ever ruffle me, I felt secure and in perfect control of myself. Thembi was gradually taking the family responsibilities and was helpful in many ways. He had become very attached to Zami, Kgatho and his sisters, he had become an idol. Then came '68 and '69 when the skies suddenly fell upon me. I lost both him and ma and I must confess that the order that had reigned in my soul almost vanished.

In her book, *Higher Than Hope*, Fatima Meer talks about Dad from interviews she had with both Rundu and Big Mommy (Mama Winnie). About Dad she says:

Thembi, alone of all Nelson's children, was old enough at the time of his imprisonment to visit him, but he never did. While members of his family have placed different interpretations on this, Winnie's explanation is as follows:

When Nelson went underground, he relied heavily on Thembi. The other children were too young to understand. Thembi almost lived underground with his father. Being of arrestable age, his father instructed him to keep an extremely low profile and not to disclose, even to his mother, his visits to Liliesleaf. I took him out there personally to spend weekends with Nelson and he joined me on many dangerous missions. His very closeness with his father and his involvement with him, forced him to maintain a façade of distance and aloofness, a façade, he maintained even in the presence of his brother, sister and his mother. I was amazed that as young as he was, he was able to keep that façade so completely. He worshipped his father and was fully committed to his role in Umkhonto. I, in, turn, worshipped Thembi.

> When he was killed in a car accident, Nelson wrote to me, where I was in the condemned cell for eighteen months in solitary confinement. He reminded me of how Thembi had visited him in Liliesleaf wearing Nelson's oversized suit jacket. He said to Nelson, 'Tata, I'm now in your place and I will try to be you and look after the family.'

I can just imagine how hurt he was by his parents' divorce. Aunt Fatima writes:

> He was old enough at the time to understand the meaning of divorce and it left him traumatised. He suffered too on account of the extreme positions his parents took, his father committed to politics, his mother to religion.

Another anecdote told to Aunt Fatima about Dad is by Rundu. Sadly, this was when their marriage was taking extreme strain. Rundu speaks of the day when things came to a head after a long period of silence between them:

> Nelson used to keep 20 cent pieces for the children to take to school. Thembi was allowed to take one 20 cent piece each morning. I had always complained that the money was too much. On this morning Thembi helped himself to two 20 cent pieces, instead of one. I scolded him and perhaps I went too far. In my anger and frustration, I must have burst out against Nelson for spoiling him. I may well have been too harsh on Thembi.
> It was after this incident that I left home and went to live with my brother. Nelson came to see me at my brother's and told me to forget the incident and return

My father

home. I returned home. I was desperate to save my marriage, even if it meant clutching at straws. But there was no thawing to the freeze. That chilling unbearable distance continued. I realised that I had no marriage. I moved out and went to live in the nurses' quarters. Perhaps I imagined that if I reversed the situation and I walked out instead of him, he would come to his senses and realise that he needed me to keep the family together. If that was the feeling, I was totally mistaken. Nelson never came to see me at the nurses' home, nor did he send messages to me. I had initiated the separation. Perhaps if I had been patient, if I had tried to understand why he had turned away from me, things may have been different, and I would still be his wife. He was the only man I ever loved. He was a wonderful husband and a wonderful father.

The children moved between us, from Orlando East to Orlando West. Maki was only two at the time, too young to understand what was going on. Makgatho at five was young enough not to be bothered by it, but Thembi, who was eight, suffered immensely.

Upon reading this excerpt, I couldn't help but think if it ever crossed Dad's mind that the 20-cent saga was not the straw that broke the camel's back, but, gathering by what Mama Winnie said about him earlier, this must have been one of the things he had to keep a façade about.

In these letters and excerpts from Aunt Fatima's book, I have finally learnt of the type of man my father was, and I believe without a shadow of doubt he would have grown to be more.

Children who grow up in single-parent families as I had, are often one dimensional in their view of life, they do not have a balanced outlook, as they tend to see things from the vantage point of the parent figure they had growing up. It's not that there is anything wrong with being one dimensional; it's just that it's not balanced.

Unlike other children who don't grow up with both parents under one roof, I never really felt I was missing something growing up without a father. Both my grandparents, Rundu and Ouma, certainly filled the void of not having a father, especially Rundu, if ever there was a void. I grew up at a time when the extended family life was very strong, as opposed to now, when the nuclear family is stronger than the extended family.

I honestly never felt there was anything missing in my life because I was growing up without a father. The environment I grew up in was not that of seeing fathers taking their daughters out for lunch, as Cofimvaba was a village town with no restaurants. Even when I went to boarding school, my friends hardly ever spoke of their fathers.

Growing up with grandmothers with strong personalities, my outlook on life had a direct bearing on my relationships with men, which is something that I tackled in my years of therapy. I realised that I am more masculine than feminine, but after becoming aware of this, I am addressing it.

I have also wondered lately if I will ever find lasting love with a man. This is the one part of my life I think has been affected the most by growing up without a father and not seeing people in love that were close to me. Children learn what they live, and since I have mostly been brought up by strong single women, where could I have seen what being in love is? I worry about this with my own children, but I guess I will allow them to walk their own paths.

I have often wondered what my life would have been like if he was still alive, especially when I went through certain challenges later in life. I certainly do know that if he had lived and was still alive, things would have been very different. For starters, I would have been very spoilt. In the few years I had with him, I know he doted on me.

There are various instances when I have thought about how he would have handled certain situations, like my first pregnancy. Would I have even fallen pregnant had he been alive? Would he have sat me down and been as candid as Granddad was about sexual health? How would he have felt about the birth of my daughter, his granddaughter, or that of Nabeela, my first grandchild and his first great-grandchild?

It is now as I reach the various milestones of my life, like turning 40 and 50 respectively, that I miss him the most. Dad would have been 70 when I turned 50 and not old by a long shot.

Chapter 5

Madiba, my grandfather

W<small>E ALL KNOW THAT</small> G<small>RANDDAD</small> was born on 18 July 1918 in Mvezo but grew up in Qunu after his father, Nkosi Mphakanyiswa, was deposed as a chief upon defying a court order.

It would be years after his release from prison that Granddad would sit us down as his grandchildren in Qunu to tell us about our heritage as Thembus. I wish we had recorded this in his voice. It was to Tatu Joyi that Granddad turned to understand the past. Tatu Joyi was his senior from the Great House of King Ngubengcuka, his great grandfather.

From the time we used to visit Cape Town with Nandi after she joined me in Cofimvaba, I was told I had a grandfather in prison. Whenever we took a drive to Table Mountain and to Sea Point, Robben Island would be pointed out to me.

I received a letter from Granddad when I turned 14. In this letter, dated 21 January 1979, he writes:

My darling Mzukulu,

It seems it was only yesterday, when on February 19 last year I sent you a card on your 13th Birthday. Again, I say, 'Many Happy Returns and a Wonderful Year'. I hope you and Nandi got the Xmas goods I sent you and that you enjoyed your Xmas. I also hope you will write and tell me everything about it.

I am told you passed your form I. Aunt Rene wrote to me from Inanda to say that this year you will be doing Form II there. I don't know whether you have succeeded in doing so. My warmest congratulations. If you are at Inanda, please tell me about the total amount of fees to be paid so that I can arrange for a scholarship.

In your last letter, you asked that I send you a leather jacket with a fur neck. I passed on your request to Khulu Winnie. She has many problems and easily forgets, but she is very kind and loves you and Nandi very much. Although she is out of work, she will struggle to send you the things you want.

I keep on thinking of 1981 which is only 2 years from now and when you will be able to visit me. I am dying to see you and I cannot wait at all for that day.

Give my love to Mom Thoko and Tata Phineas. What is his surname and address in Claremont? I wanted to send them Xmas cards, but I could not do so simply because I did not know the Claremont address.

Meanwhile, I wish this year will bring you a lot of joy and good luck.

Affectionately Khulu // To Ndindi Mandela

A lot of things strike me about this letter:
1. That Granddad managed to send my sister and me some goods. I do not remember what he sent, but I wonder where he got the money to buy these goods.
2. He was really concerned about my schooling to the point of wanting to arrange a scholarship for me.
3. That to me, it really had not sunk in that he was in prison and did not have the money to buy me things. To me, he was my grandfather and in the same way I could ask for things from Rundu and Ouma, I could ask for them from him.
4. That he was trying to shield the truth from me about the police brutality against Mama Winnie.

I do remember that I was to go to Inanda Seminary when I passed my Form I, but something happened that angered Rundu and I ended up not going. It was not something I did, but more along the lines of funds not being available on time to pay for my tuition, and I ended up going to Nyanga High School.

Granddad and I wrote to each other often in the two years preceding my first visit with him. By this time, he had started to write to Nandi as well on her birthdays. All his letters ended the same way: *A million Kisses & tons & tons of Love. Affectionate, Khulu.*

The big year – 1981 – came. I could not wait for the June vacation so I could see my grandfather at last. Finally, the schools closed, and we were off to Cape Town with Nandi, although she wouldn't come to the prison with me, as you had to be 16 years old to qualify for a visit. The visit was to be on a weekend, Saturday and Sunday, 30 minutes each day. The dates were 27 and 28 June 1981.

Can you imagine how inexcusable apartheid laws were?

Here I was not having seen Granddad from the day I was born, and I was to catch up with him in only an hour, cumulatively. How do you cram 16 years of your story into one hour?

Ouma drove me to the docks in what is now known as the Victoria and Alfred Wharf. Aunt Maki had warned me not to go below deck, as I would be nauseous. I was both excited and nervous – this would be my very first boat ride. Cape Town is cold and miserable in winter and, lo and behold, on the day of my visit it was dreary and drizzling. I had no choice but to stay below deck. The waters were choppy but, fortunately, due to my excitement I did not get nauseous. We reached Robben Island, a place that used to be pointed out to me in hushed tones from Lion's Head. I was ushered into a cold waiting room.

Finally, a guard came to get me, as it was time for my visit. I was ushered into a room that had partitions with small glass panels and an intercom. Granddad was sitting in the second-last cubicle. Years later Aunt Zindzi told me that they did this so you could not tell people from outside how tall he was. Lieutenant Gregory was the warder who was with him on that first visit. He came close to the window so we could touch opposite sides of it as a form of embracing. We both kissed the glass as well. This would be our routine greeting during all of the non-contact visits.

I was a bit nervous at first, as I did not know that the warder would be listening in – no one had explained this to me. I guess it must have been something difficult to explain for Aunt Maki. I had to experience it. Granddad had the ability to make anyone relax and 10 minutes into the visit we were chatting like we'd been seeing each other for years. He asked me about school, what subjects I was doing and which ones I liked. What were my aspirations? We were doing well until he asked me if I had a boyfriend. I tensed up, as this was a taboo subject in Rundu's household back in Cofimvaba. Jehovah's Witnesses hold a belief that you can only court just before marriage. He also asked me if I had had my pap smear yet. I had no clue what a pap smear was. How wet behind the ears I was! Before I knew it, the visit was over, but I was not worried, as I was coming back the next day.

We were five minutes late to get to the docks that Sunday and as Ouma stopped the car I could still see the foam the ferry had left behind. I was sobbing and did not even want to eat when we got back to Retreat. On Monday afternoon Ouma received a telegram that I was to go for my missed visit on the Wednesday. To say I was overjoyed is an understatement. What we talked about on that day is a blur, but at the end of the visit Gregory handed me a wrapped gift from Granddad, which I only opened when I reached Ouma's house in Retreat. Under the gift wrapping was a box of Black Magic chocolates with a message that said, 'Your visit will always be a bittersweet memory, Love Khulu.' I can still see the cover of this box of chocolates – it was white and glossy with a single red rose. It was years before I understood the message.

Later, when I knew about dark chocolates, I understood the paradox of bittersweet. More importantly, I got to learn through some of the letters that Granddad wrote to a number of people after Dad's death that he was 16 years old the last time Granddad had seen him alive, the same age I was when I went to visit Granddad the first time. It was bittersweet indeed.

The relationship and the bond we shared during that first visit were amazing. It was like I had known and talked to him all my life. I could talk to him about anything. When re-reading the letter I wrote to him as soon as I returned to Cofimvaba, I can't help but laugh at my openness with him.

It reads:

Dear Khulu

I am in a good condition; hope you are also in a good one.

I hope you won't be very much disappointed about my failure in the June exams. I did my best but to no avail. I told you about the situation of the school and I think you will understand. I don't want to be here again. Nandi passed her exams, she was no. 5.

Ouma gave me your photo, I think you were still young at the photo, wearing boxing gloves.

You know I never had much time discussing with Mom, because Dad [was] there and I didn't tell her all the things you said, I must say. Dad is a bit strict. He is an old-fashioned father. When he calls me he expects me to be frightened [and] run to him like he is a giant, that's where we quarrel. I understand when he calls me, I must attend to him quickly and respect him. How should I respect him when he is like that?

When he is in Cape Town, we go to no activities. I mean, we are young and want something to freshen our minds. To him it seems as if we must stay at home and work. We go out only during Christmas.

Mama, I think is a bit afraid of him because she won't say anything though we are her kids. Ouma said you encouraged Mom to marry again. If she wasn't married, we would live nice and have everything that teenagers have.

Next time I write you, I'll be sending you my photo too. Pass my regards to Tata Sisulu.

Your Granddaughter
Ndindi

I had just turned 16 when I wrote this letter. I wonder what was going on in his mind when he read it. I honestly do not understand where, at 16, I got the notion that Mom was scared of my stepdad. The rest, however, does sound like me. I now understand when Aunt Linda Zama tells me that Granddad used to say to her, 'You know Linda, Nandi is a lady, but Ndindi is a rascal.'

The following year, April 1982, after contracting TB, Granddad was transferred to Pollsmoor Maximum Security Prison, together with the other Rivonia trialists. His letters and my visits continued like clockwork. Pollsmoor Prison was much closer to Retreat, where Ouma had a house. At times she would just wait for me in the car until the visit was over. The visiting times at Pollsmoor were also extended to an hour, but they were still non-contact visits.

My visit to him in June 1984 remains etched in my memory. By now, I had been seeing him regularly and knew the Pollsmoor visiting routine off by heart. You come in, you register at the front desk and you are taken to the waiting room while they go and call him. You're then ushered into a room with similar cubicles as in Robben Island and you kiss and touch through the glass. I know it sounds so cold, but if you are the progeny of a political prisoner these 'abnormal' situations stop bothering you and they seem normal.

During this visit, though, I was taken to a different waiting area that looked more like an office. It had a desk, two armchairs and some office stuff. I was asked to sit and wait. After about five minutes, the warder came in followed by Granddad. We hugged and held each other for what seemed like a lifetime. To this day, I can't begin to explain how it felt to touch him for the first time. He was so tall. The one thing that marred the visit is that at 19 I had discovered I was pregnant, and Aunt Maki, who had visited him the week prior to my visit, had told him. I was not showing yet and I knew he would be disappointed. We talked about my pregnancy and he asked me how far along I was. I told him I was 16 weeks pregnant.

Although he was disappointed, he blamed himself for my pregnancy. He told me he felt it was his fault for being absent in my life and not being able to guide me when it came to sex. He added that because he knew Rundu's religious beliefs, he knew that the subject of sex and boyfriends was taboo. I knew it was not Rundu's fault. One thing was clear, though – he wanted me to continue with my studies as soon as my son was born.

On 27 November 1984 I gave birth to Tembela Thembisile Mandela. Tembela would be a year and a half before Granddad met him and that was in June 1986. Again, it would be years later that I would learn how he felt about Tembela, how he looked forward to seeing him, as he was his first great-grandson. I would read about his feelings in a calendar he kept in his cell. Granddad had a habit of writing everything on his calendar. I had brought Tembela with me on my first visit to him that June. The rules in Pollsmoor were beginning to be relaxed since the contact visit. Although I did not bring Tembela the second day, he did not say much about it, but I was to read years later in the archives kept at the Nelson Mandela Foundation how disappointed he was.

On 7 December 1988 Granddad was transferred to Victor Verster Prison. Victor Verster was much more relaxed and we could spend the whole day with him. When I went to visit him in late December the same year, he gave me a letter to deliver to Mr Trevor Manuel, who was under house arrest. I loved the house he was in. My memory of this house is a bit fuzzy, but I remember I was dropped off by Ouma and stayed for about two hours. At this point, I knew what he was imprisoned for. I guess I deleted the information from my mind subconsciously so as not to remember anything in case I was to be interrogated. Such is the life of children of political prisoners.

In June 1989, our whole family went to visit Granddad in Victor Verster. Mama Winnie; Aunt Zindzi; Uncle Makgatho with his children and wife, Aunt Zondi; Aunt Maki with her children; Nandi and me with our children – we all descended upon Victor Verster. He had called all of us to tell us that they, the political prisoners, particularly the Rivonia trialists, would be released unconditionally and that the ANC was to be unbanned. Grandpa Sisulu and the other Rivonia trialists would be released first, and Granddad would be the last to be released.

I had mixed emotions towards this news. Part of me did not know what to expect, but a large part of me was elated that I was to have him to myself at last. To me it meant he would be free to go shopping with me, have coffee or go to picnics – pretty much like how my relationship was with Rundu.

Boy, was I wrong!

After Khulu Sisulu was released in October 1989, I knew Granddad's release was imminent. That year he had arranged a scholarship for me to go to MEDUNSA to do a degree in nursing through the South African Council of Churches.

In late January 1990 I journeyed to Ga-Rankuwa in Pretoria to register and commence my studies. On Sunday, 11 February 1990, I woke up as per usual and got busy with my routine of finishing my assignments and bits and pieces of this and that. I had a small TV in my room, the room I shared with Sibongile Guma. I think it was Sibongile who asked me to turn the TV on, as she'd heard in the dining hall that Granddad was about to be released. Lo and behold, when we did, a crowd had started to gather outside Victor Verster Prison. It was like a circus. Cell phones were still new those days and I did not have one to call my aunt and ask her anything.

The reporters kept updating the audience each time the release time changed. By now, we could hear singing coming from the amphitheatre we had at MEDUNSA. We switched off our TV and joined the growing crowd at the amphitheatre, where we watched the proceedings on a bigger screen. After he walked out with Mama Winnie with his fist up in the air, the crowd at the amphitheatre broke out in song and we marched all the way from Ga-Rankuwa to Mamelodi.

The ANC held a welcoming rally for him at the FNB stadium soon after that. MEDUNSA organised about 10 buses to take students to the rally. By the time we arrived at the FNB stadium, it was filled to capacity and they were not allowing any more people inside. So, we climbed onto the stands in the stadium from outside and by the time we reached the top where some of us could get a glimpse of what was happening inside, Granddad was being driven in and the stadium came alive. People were standing and dancing on the stands so much so that the whole stadium was shaking. I was scared I would fall off but that did not stop me from trying to dance too.

It would be three months before I would see Granddad as a free man and that was the beginning of our strained relationship. I had illusions that when he was finally released, I would have easy access to him. I soon realised that not only was he my grandfather – no, my father, such was the role he played in my life – he was also a grandfather to millions around the world. Even when I finally saw him after three months, there was none of the privacy and intimacy we had while he was in prison.

I had arrived at his house in Vilakazi Street in the early afternoon, after catching two commuter minibus taxis from MEDUNSA. He was in meetings and I only got to see him late in the evening for about 10 minutes. I was both disappointed and hurt. I went back to Ga-Rankuwa late on Sunday with a heavy heart. After that, I must have visited him two more times. The last time I visited him was shortly before we wrote our year-end exams. By this time, they had moved to the big house, also in Soweto but a mere stone's throw away from the one in Vilakazi Street. We called this house Parliament, owing to its size and because most meetings happened there.

After my first year at MEDUNSA, I packed up to go home to Durban, where I lived with Mom. Tembela, aged 6, was living with her at the time as well. I had made up my mind that I would not be returning to MEDUNSA. My reasons for not returning were born out of frustration. The scholarship Granddad had got me was not a full one. It necessitated that I receive a stipend for toiletries and the only person I could turn to regarding this was Granddad, only he had no time, as he was attending to matters of the country. I had been working since Tembela was born and was therefore self-reliant, and I could not stomach this relegation to child status. I had a profession. If Granddad wanted me to stay at varsity with no means of support from him, he was sadly mistaken. So, I quit without telling him, which earned me his anger. Well, he had earned mine first.

I went back to work at St Aidan's Hospital in Durban as an ICU nurse. I saw Granddad again at Aunt Zindzi's wedding to Mr Zweli Hlongwane in 1992, as I was one of her bridesmaids. Throughout this time, my relationship with Granddad remained strained.

In 1993, at the age of 28, I fell pregnant with my daughter

and last born, Pumla. She was born on 16 November 1993. At the time of Pumla's birth, the house Granddad had bought Nandi and me in Westville, Durban, was still being transferred into our names. We moved in shortly before our first democratic elections.

After the ANC won the elections, there was to be an inauguration – something we'd never heard of before – and not only that, I was to attend this auspicious occasion. It still did not click that my grandfather, Nelson Rolihlahla Mandela, was to be the first democratically elected president of South Africa. The same person who had been deemed a terrorist a few years before. This was surreal in so many ways. For the first time I was to rub shoulders with and be in the same audience as people I had only seen on TV.

Nandi and I flew from Durban the night before to sleep at Granddad's house in Houghton. 27 April 1994 came, with clear blue skies. We were driven to the presidential house in Pretoria to wait until it was time for us to be seated. We were to be seated last, as we were to sit on the podium. While we waited, Granddad came in briefly to greet all of us and was soon ushered away. I must confess, as we were all given a tour around the house, part of me still thought it was a dream. The house was too large and seemed cold. It had none of the cosiness of Cofimvaba or Houghton.

After Granddad was sworn in, we were taken back to Bryntirion Estate (as it is now called) where there was a marquee set up for lunch for VIP guests. Later that evening, as I was walking through the house, I tripped and sprained my ankle. I was taken to 1 Military Hospital for X-rays to establish if I had fractured any bones, which I had not. The ankle was bandaged and the next day Nandi and I flew back to Durban.

After Granddad became president, it was even harder to

see him, as his schedule was extremely busy. I can count the occasions I spent time with him during his presidential years on my fingers. That was how much we became disconnected from each other. Besides that, those who had previously ignored him when he was imprisoned were now suddenly 'new' friends. On occasion, I did meet famous people, like Fidel Castro at the home in Houghton. That was a memorable meeting. President Castro had come with his grandchildren and watching these two luminaries talking like old men surrounded by their kin was extraordinary. It is a pity that this was before cell phones had cameras, because I would have taken pictures of that.

Another reason I don't have much to say about Granddad as President is that, to me, he never changed from being my grandfather. I do not remember even a single time when I felt like pinching myself because he was now head of state. I guess this owes to my upbringing by Rundu of viewing everyone equally and not according to their station.

Towards the end of his presidency, we had a huge fall out and were not even on speaking terms. This time it was bad and unlike our other disagreements, which were all reconciable. I even boycotted his 80th birthday, his announcement that he was marrying Mama Graça and his farewell party as the president. I had met Mama Graça around 1996, when Granddad was attending the African Peace Award in Durban. He had asked to see Nandi and me and was staying at the Maharani Hotel. When we came, he introduced us to Mama Graça. I guess he wanted us to like her, and we did.

Because of how I was brought up, I was unfazed and never thought of myself as the granddaughter of the first black president of South Africa. I actually still don't, which is why it used to come as a surprise to me that when I became active on social media, some of the statements I made on my timeline would end up being front-page news. My rape story, or the fact that I spoke about my concerns about the ANC not upholding the principles of the founding fathers of the organisation back in 2016, became news.

Nelson Rolihlahla Mandela was my grandfather, period, not the president of the ANC and not the president of the country. I related to him on those terms and those terms only. Being brought up by a devout Jehovah's Witness, I was raised with an extremely strong sense of revering God above anyone else on the planet. Granddad being president was not my accolade, but his, and that also meant people did not have to treat me in any particular way, or at least, that is how I felt and still do. It is only when people start saying that 'Nelson Mandela sold out' that I get really upset.

I also never felt the brunt of apartheid until later in life, certainly not while I was growing up in Cofimvaba. I had left Orlando East at the age of seven, in 1972, before I was able to notice any discrimination. I became aware of the political climate at Nyanga High School and when I visited Mom in Durban.

In 2000, I relocated to Johannesburg with my children, as I had been promoted by Prime Cure, a group of privately owned primary health care clinics, and the position was based in their Johannesburg marketing division. I had been working with the group from 1996, as a community nurse, in the Durban area. I sold the house Granddad had since bought me in Pinetown, leaving Nandi to be the sole owner of the house he had bought for us both in Westville. I bought a house in Randpark Ridge, as Pumla had started Grade One at Randpark Primary and Tembela was to attend Northcliff High. By this time our relationship was on better footing. As he was no longer president, access to him was much easier.

When Mom died in 2002, Granddad stepped up and became like a father to Nandi, my other two siblings and me. Not only did he make a huge contribution towards the funeral expenses, he made sure that after the lunch he came back with us, to the home in Claremont where Mom was staying, to make sure we were okay. I had never seen him so helpless. I could see in his eyes that he wished he could take away our pain.

Rundu died in 2004 on 30 April. After her funeral I went off the rails into a deep depression for which I had to go to therapy. I was in therapy for three years, during which time I dealt with my daddy/granddad issues. During the period of 2004 to 2010, our relationship grew stronger (more on this later).

I got to know his wit and his subtle way of putting people in their place. This I had learnt two years earlier when we attended Josina's wedding in Maputo before Mom's death. Josina is Mama Graça's daughter with Samora Machel. As we all know, Mozambique is a Portuguese-speaking country. At Josina's church wedding, speaker upon speaker was addressing the guests in Portuguese with no one translating for the English speakers. The time came for Granddad to speak as the stepfather of the bride. No sooner had he taken to the podium to speak than Mama Graça's brother went to stand next to him to translate into Portuguese. So, Granddad started his speech and as he paused, Mama Graça's brother started translating, at which point he stopped him and said, 'You can translate when I'm done.' He then made such a long speech that Mama Graça's brother sat down, as there would be no point translating. We were chuckling, as we knew what message he was sending.

Granddad also had a wicked sense of humour and he would often poke fun at himself. He would tell us of the time he started dating and was not adept at using a knife and fork. The girl he was dating came from a sophisticated family, as he put it. He was invited to join her family at the dinner table. He said every time he tried to cut the meat, the piece of meat would elude him and move all around the plate to the extent that he told them he was not hungry anymore, as he did not want to embarrass himself. He said to me, 'You know, darling, I think they gave me the toughest piece of meat just to prove I was not fit to date this girl.'

Another time he told me about the first time he came to Johannesburg and was mentored by Grandpa Sisulu. He says when he first met Mr Oliver Tambo, at the reception was an African woman typing. Not only was it his first time seeing this, it was also his first time seeing anyone typing without looking at the keyboard.

He also had a very naughty side to him. Whenever I brought any of my male friends who had asked to see him, he would tease me mercilessly. As soon as we sat down, I would ask him to behave. I would see it coming as he'd have a glint in his eyes followed by his boyish smile, and he would ask my friend, 'Did my granddaughter propose to you?' and burst out laughing. I miss this banter we had.

Sometimes I would find him listening to a battered old transistor radio at the dining room table. This was a man who had more than one TV in his house. The simplicity of how he lived his life is something of a marvel to me. Or the way he would just want to eat *umvubo* (sour milk and mealie pap) when every cuisine his heart desired could be prepared for him at the blink of an eye.

Granddad had a certain vanity about him. He would keep a small comb in the breast pocket of his shirt to comb his hair whenever he went to the bathroom. I would tease him by asking if he was expecting an attractive visitor he wanted to look good for and he would find this very funny. He loved it when I called him handsome. I would come in and greet him with, 'Morning handsome' and he would smile like a little boy.

He was also very strict. We were in Qunu during one of the December holidays. We had a tradition of choosing a night before we all went back to our respective homes to have our Christmas dinner. On this evening, we had told him that the dinner would be ready at 7 pm but, for some reason or other, it was not. We were scuttling around like headless chickens when we heard the lift coming down, promptly at 7 pm. He went straight for his chair and sat down. After about 15 or so minutes of gathering everyone to come and sit down, we could tell he was annoyed. His upper lip had the biggest pout you can imagine. He was also hungry, as he'd spared his appetite for dinner. Now, one thing you must never do is to starve the Madiba clan. We are nasty people when hungry.

After we had all sat down, Mama Graça asked him to address us as the patriarch of the family. He went off on us about how rude it is to be late and how people will never take us seriously if we turn up late for meetings. Mama Graça tried to pacify him by telling him that we were on holiday, but he would have none of it. Thankfully, by mid-dinner his spirits had lifted.

Ebeyingcathu ekutyeni uMadiba, he watched his diet like a hawk. One of the things I take after him is that trait and his love for exercise. He exercised regularly. He had a wheel, a fitness apparatus, to get rid of the pot belly that he used to tell his medical staff about. Mama Xoli would tell us that whenever she cooked lasagne and he would see even the slightest amount of fat on his plate, he would call her and point to his plate and uMama would know what he meant.

I also got to know how close Granddad was to his mother, to the extent that we used to call him a mommy's boy behind his back. In all the stories that he would tell us, he always spoke of his mother, never his father. He told us of when, on his graduation at Fort Hare, he refused to go into the graduation hall until his mother could attend. We were having lunch one day, and I asked him why he had not given Mandla's first wife *igama lasemzini* after his mother, Nosekeni, and instead gave her his father's third wife's name, Nodayimani. It is customary in the Thembu and Xhosa tradition to give a new name to a woman who gets married into the family as a way of welcoming her. The name usually has a correspondence to her role in the family. He pondered and was pensive for a moment before uttering, 'That name is sacred.' I was floored and understood that day the depth of how he felt about my great-grandmother.

Although I don't know much about my great-grandmother, the little I do know tells me she had a profound impact on Granddad. I know she was born around 1851, but because registration of births was not common back then the exact date is unclear. She was the daughter of Nkedama from the amaMpemvu clan, hence she was known as umamMpemvu. It is customary in our culture as African people for a married woman to be known or called by her clan name versus her maiden surname. She bore my great-grandfather Chief Mphakanyiswa Gadla four children: Baliwe Mandela, Rolihlahla Mandela (Nelson is the name Granddad was given by his teacher when he started school), Mabel Notancu Timakhwe (née Mandela) and Leabie Constance Mbekeni (née Mandela).

Rundu was also in awe of her. In one of the interviews she granted Fatima Meer, for *Higher Than Hope*, Rundu had this to say:

In 1949, Nelson's eldest sister wrote to say that their mother was unwell. Nelson arranged for her to come to Johannesburg to see medical specialists. She stayed with us after that and filled our house, providing it with a gentle authority and giving it the dignity of the older generation which it lacked. She was weak and distraught on arrival but gained strength quite rapidly. We got on very well together and Makhulu (Mother) was a great help with housework and children.

Then there's a story told by Mama Graça that upon returning from school Granddad told his mother his 'new' name and she said, 'Oh! Nelisini!' Ukhokho (great-grandparent), as we say in isiXhosa, must have seen some potential in all her children, for she made sure they were all educated. I see strength in her in the picture I have of her and in pictures of her outside court during the Rivonia trial.

Granddad told a story that once when his mom had visited him in Johannesburg prior to the Rivonia trial, he had bought her a lot of clothes and a coat. He had really spoiled her, and this was perhaps his way of taking care of her the way he felt a son should take care of a mother. One thing I certainly know is that he had regrets whenever he spoke about her. He felt he had not looked after her as a son should have. I also think that this stems from the fact that he was her only son.

There was another incident pertaining to his mother in 2012, in Qunu, on Granddad's birthday. Bhut Bantu Holomisa had come to visit just before we had his birthday lunch. They had both been sitting in the upstairs TV room when Bhut Bantu came to call me. He told me that Granddad had told him he missed his mother and wanted to go see her. I was taken aback by this request and worried at the same time, as his memory had been fading. I was wondering if he'd forgotten that his mother had died when he was in prison. I asked Bhut Bantu this and he told me he understood that and all he wanted to do was to visit her grave. By this time, he had become very frail. We were worried about how we would get him there, as the road to her grave was not good and the journey, albeit it only a few metres from the house, would be difficult for him. In any event, we arranged with the security personnel to make this slow journey across the street to her grave. We drove as close as we could to where he could at least see the headstone. He was wheelchair bound at this point. He did not say a word. He just sat in quiet reflection and after about 10 to 15 minutes told us we could take him back.

I have often wondered about this visit. This was a year and a half before his own death. What was going on in his mind? Was it his own way of alerting his mother that he would be joining her soon? Perhaps he wanted to lay his demons, the regrets he had about her, finally to rest.

It's funny how, as people age, they seem to revert to an almost child-like state. Granddad was no different. At times he would point-blank refuse to take his treatment. I would find his medical team cajoling him and calling him by his clan names to coax him into taking it, especially if Mama Graça was away. He would also refuse to eat and say he'd been eating for the past 93 years and that he didn't have to eat.

Towards the end of his life, he and I became very close. After he was taken to Qunu early in 2012, I resolved to spend at least one long weekend with him there a month. I would fly to Mthatha on a Thursday and leave on a Monday. Around this time, his short-term memory was failing, as is common with people his age, and he would not remember if he was in Johannesburg or Qunu. During one of the weekends I was visiting, he had one such memory lapse. The previous night everything had been fine. I was in my room and it was mid-morning when Madlamini came to call me, as Granddad was sitting in the kitchen (this was very unusual for him), refusing to leave. I went to the kitchen to find out what was happening, and he asked me, 'Darling, where are we?' Me: 'We're in Qunu, Granddad.' We argued back and forth and had to call his cousin Grandpa Sitsheketshe, who he knew lived in Qunu, to convince him. While we were waiting for him to arrive, he looked at me with such anger and said, 'I never knew my own granddaughter could do this to me!'

During such instances, my heart would break. This was the man I had known at his strongest and I was now seeing him at his weakest. Granddad battled with his frailties. It took him the longest time to accept using a walker and then finally the wheelchair. Whenever the walker would be brought to him after breakfast, for example, you would see that he was willing his legs to carry him and not use the walker. At times, he would say, 'My legs are refusing to obey me.'

One morning I had gone to the house in Houghton to have breakfast with him and the walker was brought to him so we could sit in the living room. The nurses would first pull the chair out of the table to position it in such a way that it was easy to manoeuvre him to the walker. I pre-empted this by telling him that we were going to the living room so he could read his papers. The nurse pulled out his chair, but something annoyed him, and he told the nurse that I would take him to the living room. Now I got worried because he was tall and heavy, and I knew we would both buckle under his weight. He tried to stand up and couldn't, but as soon as the nurses advanced, he got more annoyed and said, '*Voetsek!* – which was the biggest swear word in his vocabulary. I wanted so much to laugh at this but knew I could not risk it. Finally, I told the medical team to stand behind me, away from his line of vision and his peripheral vision (his peripheral vision was excellent). They did so and I asked him to stand up while simultaneously asking the nurses to advance with his walker. After 15 minutes of cajoling we managed to have him seated in the living room.

I cherish the times spent with him towards the end of his life, from 2011 until his death, more than the times before that. It's not that we talked a lot – that happened when he was in prison. At times we would sit, whether in Qunu or Houghton, him reading his papers, me either reading a book or working on my iPad. Without talking, he'd suddenly extend his hand and we would touch. He'd squeeze my hand for a while and then let go. No words were needed; we seemed to have developed a certain non-verbal communication.

It would get difficult to leave him, especially if I had been to visit him in Qunu. There used to be only two flights to Mthatha per day from Johannesburg, one in the morning and another late in the afternoon. I would leave on the afternoon flight. The flight would be at 5:55 pm and at 3 pm we would start our jive with him. I would go to the formal lounge where he'd be reading his papers and tell him that I was about to leave, and he'd act as if he did not hear me. I would have to wait until he had released me by saying, 'Okay, darling.' Sometimes this would take half an hour. It was, however, different if we were in Johannesburg.

Our goodbyes would go something like this:

Me: 'Granddad, I have to go but I'll come see you on Wednesday.'

Him: 'What day is it today?'

Me: 'It's Monday, Granddad.'

He'd sit and ponder this before releasing me with his

usual 'Okay, darling'. I would then kiss him and leave.

There is one particular memory I wish I could freeze in time. It was during one of my visits to Qunu in September 2012. We were sitting in the living room next to his bedroom when one of the members of the medical team suggested we watch a video. I settled on a documentary called *Nelson Mandela – The Journey*. It had been one of my dreams to go to the movies with him. Although this was not the same, it was just fine. I was sitting on the floor with my head on his lap as we watched this documentary. When Christo Brandt appeared on the screen narrating how on the day Granddad received the news of my father's death, upon walking past his cell in Robben Island, he'd found him huddled in a corner with his blanket wrapped around his shoulders as if he was wrapping his pain around himself. I felt him become tense. I held his hand and he eased up and we continued to watch the documentary. This memory rates among the best I have of our times together.

When he fell seriously ill in Qunu, in December 2012, I feared the worst. From the first time he got ill and was admitted at Milpark Hospital in January 2011, the nurse in me knew it was the beginning of the end, which is the reason why I took a sabbatical to spend as much time as I could with him before he transitioned to another realm. I had done the same with Rundu. I did not want to have regrets after his death.

Granddad was a fighter. Shortly after Christmas, he was discharged, and it was good to have him home. By the grace of God and a team of exceptional doctors, we were able to spend more time with him. He was now extremely frail and had gone into a more reflective mode as he transitioned. He would have bad days and good days. Mid-May 2013, on one of the good days, we were sitting in the TV room in Houghton. It was one of those May days where the sun was out and it was a bit warm. He had been cooped up in the house for a very long time. Suddenly he grew restless. I asked him what he wanted and he said he wanted to sit outside in the garden. He was in his wheelchair and it would be easy to move him. I asked the medical team to assist me to take him to the front garden. When we went outside, all he did was lift his head up and bask in the sun, and he would occasionally watch the trees as they swayed from side to side in the wind. We sat in the garden for about half an hour and then had to take him inside, as the sun was beginning to set and there was a cold draft.

When he was being wheeled into the house, he said 'I want to go home.' I understood perfectly what he meant – home meant Qunu. Granddad wanted to take his last breath among his ancestors. Sadly, this was not to be, as two weeks later, on 8 June 2013, he was admitted to hospital yet again and this time around I knew he might not return home alive.

On 18 July 2013, we all spent his last birthday with him in hospital. Later that day, he slipped into unconsciousness. From that day on, he would flit in and out of consciousness. I spent my days in a daze travelling to and from the hospital. Some days, I would leave the hospital very late with Granddad hanging onto life by a thread, expecting to receive a call in the morning that he had passed on. In the morning I would drive to the hospital with my heart in my throat, not knowing what to expect when I got there. At times I would arrive to find him looking much better. As an ICU nurse, I knew the nature of the beast we were dealing with.

There were a lot of things that overwhelmed me during Granddad's last admissions to Mediclinic Heart Hospital in Pretoria from June 2013. On 8 June 2013, when he got admitted, there was a restriction of visitors, as the doctors wanted to stabilise him before the rest of the family could visit. Since I'm the eldest grandchild, I was allowed to be among the first round of family to visit. I will never forget the amount of media that awaited us upon leaving. All I could hear was the click of cameras, as if we were on the red carpet. I had never seen anything like it. There was a day I read a newsfeed that seemed to time how long I had been inside the hospital. What was overwhelming about all this attention was the speculation about him. It hurt to read news predicting his death and saying the most horrific things about a person I loved dearly. Yes, I understood the interest in him, but that did not stop him from being a father, a grandfather and a great-grandfather. It was hard for us to shield our children and the younger ones in our family from the malicious news that sometimes reported he was already dead. Some publications even reported that he had died, and we were artificially keeping him alive.

It was a mad time. One day we were asked to pick up flowers and messages left by well-wishers outside the hospital. The media mobbed us and, at some point, we thought they were going to crush us as they clamoured all around. After that day, we asked the Nelson Mandela Foundation to collect the flowers and messages for us.

The general public was amazing. Granddad had a way of uniting people. I saw my country united in prayer for him. Those prayers gave us strength; they fortified me. I will be eternally grateful for the strength South Africans gave me.

When he was discharged from hospital in September 2013, I breathed a sigh of relief because that meant he would be closer to visit. The commute between Pretoria and Johannesburg was taking a toll on me. I largely neglected my children, as I had to concentrate all my energies on him. He was still drifting in and out of consciousness, although he could tell voices apart. When I visited, I would sit and hold his now very frail hand, but even then, I had to wait for him to dismiss me when it was time to go home. If he had not dismissed me, I could tell because when I told him I was leaving he would hold tight and not let go.

It broke my heart to see this proud Thembu man at his weakest. I must be honest, by November 2013, I found myself praying that God would end his suffering, but I knew it was not up to me but between him and God. We each have our own covenant with God and, in the end, he had to find peace that his covenant with God was not complete yet.

A month after that, on 5 December 2013 at 9:50 pm, Granddad took his last breath, surrounded by his family at our home in Houghton.

Chapter 6

Evelyn, my grandmother

RUNDU WAS BORN ON 18 MAY 1922 in the village of Qutubeni, and she was the last born. Her father, a mine worker, died when she was an infant, leaving her mother with six children to raise single-handedly. Three of her siblings died while she was still in infancy and her mother died when she was 12, leaving her and her sister Kate under the care of their older brother, Sam Mase. Khulu Sam was a devout Christian and had a close friendship with his cousin Walter Sisulu. They went to school together. In 1928, Khulu Walter moved to Soweto and obtained a house in Orlando East. Later, he was joined by Sam. Khulu Ntsompoyi, as we called him, was becoming politicised and thus encouraged Khulu Sisulu to read left-wing literature and join the ANC.

In 1939, Rundu joined her brother and cousin to train as a nurse at Hillbrow hospital, fulfilling the wishes of her mother. There she befriended Khulu Walter's girlfriend, Albertina, whom he had met in 1941 and would marry in 1944. When Khulu Walter and Khulu Albertina moved to

Evelyn, my grandmother

a larger house at 7372 Orlando West, they gave their older house to Sam. Rundu and Khulu Ntsompoyi continued to visit the Sisulus at their new house and met their lodger, Nelson Mandela.

Soon after Rundu's arrival in Soweto, her brother Sam got married and was allocated a house in Orlando East. She went to live with him but continued to be a regular visitor at the Sisulus, where she met Granddad. She recounts for Aunt Fatima:

I think I loved him the first time I saw him. The Sisulus had many friends. They were such genial, generous people and Walter had lots of friends who came to their home, but there was something very special about Nelson. Within days of our first meeting, we were going steady and within months he proposed. Nelson spoke to my brother and he was overjoyed, the Sisulus were overjoyed. Everyone we knew said we made a very good couple. We were radiant on the day of our marriage which took place at the Native Commissioner's Court in Johannesburg. We could not afford a wedding feast. That was in 1944.

Looking at the dates now, I believe Rundu was already pregnant by the time she got married, as Dad, their firstborn, was born on 23 February 1945. They named their son Thembekile Madiba Mandela. Needing more space as their family grew, they moved to a two-roomed house – 719 Orlando East – for several months before relocating to 8115 Orlando West early in 1947. Granddad's mother, Great-Grandma Nosekeni, got on well with Rundu, who said of her mother-in-law:

I am Ndileka

> *Makhulu's presence gave me the opportunity to take a more active interest in the Nursing Union. I had been roped into the union by Adelaide, who later married Oliver Tambo. Adelaide was vivacious and very persuasive. She and Gladys Khala had strong feelings about the rights of nurses and particularly about the discriminatory wages of Black Nurses. I shared those feelings and I threw in my weight with them.*
>
> *We settled into a happy family. Nelson was a highly organised person and very regular in his habits. He was up at the crack of dawn, jogged a few miles, had a light breakfast and was off for the day. He liked doing the family shopping and I was more than happy for him to do so. He enjoyed bathing the babies in the evenings and there were occasions when he took over the cooking from us women.*

I started living with Rundu at the age of two and she became my mother in every way that counts for me. My mother was more like an affectionate aunt I visited from time to time. I commend both my parents for loving me enough to realise I would be better placed with Rundu than with them.

I do not know for sure why exactly led Rundu to move to Cofimvaba in the Eastern Cape, nor do I remember asking her. All I know is that three years after she buried her son, my father, in 1969, we moved to Cofimvaba. I also know that that decision altered the trajectory of my life and I am better for it.

I think the next excerpt from *Higher Than Hope* could perhaps provide a little clarity as to why Rundu chose to relocate not only to the Eastern Cape but to Cofimvaba specifically. She tells Aunt Fatima the following: '*We had many visitors, especially from the Transkei. They came and*

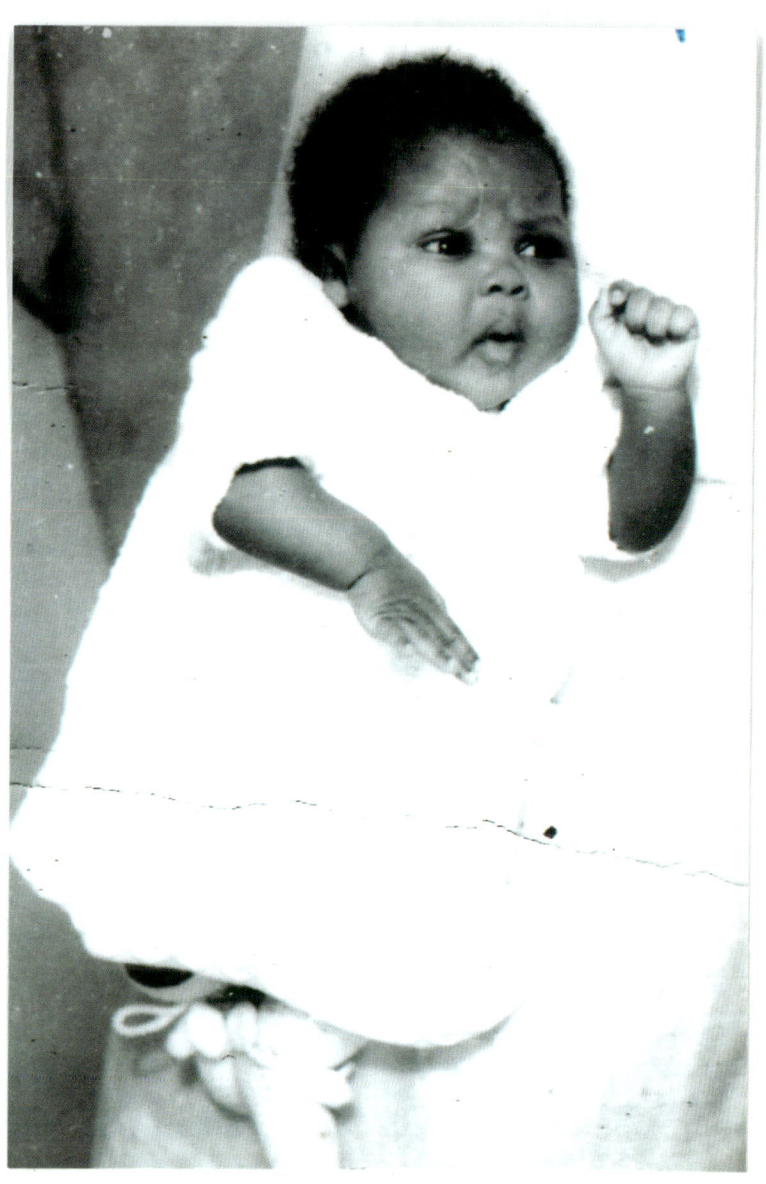

The only image I have of me as an infant

Top right: Sis Thembeka at home looking after Mandla, Nobuntu, Saziso, Tukwini, Phumeza, Nandi and Mongameli

Top left: A family portrait of all the cousins I grew up with posing with Aunt Maki and Sis Nomakhaya (seated)

Bottom right: (Left–right) Matshezi (Samuel's wife), Samuel (Rundu's brother) and Rundu

Bottom left: My cousins and I posing for a picture after coming back from playing outside

Top: Aunt Maki's graduation at Fort Hare. Standing from left: Me, Maki, Rundu and Nandi. Seated from left: Siyabulela, Tukwini, Viwe and Dumani

Bottom: Rundu (on the far right) with friends working as a student nurse

Top: The house in Cofimvaba where I grew up

Bottom: Maziyavuza Store in Cofimvaba

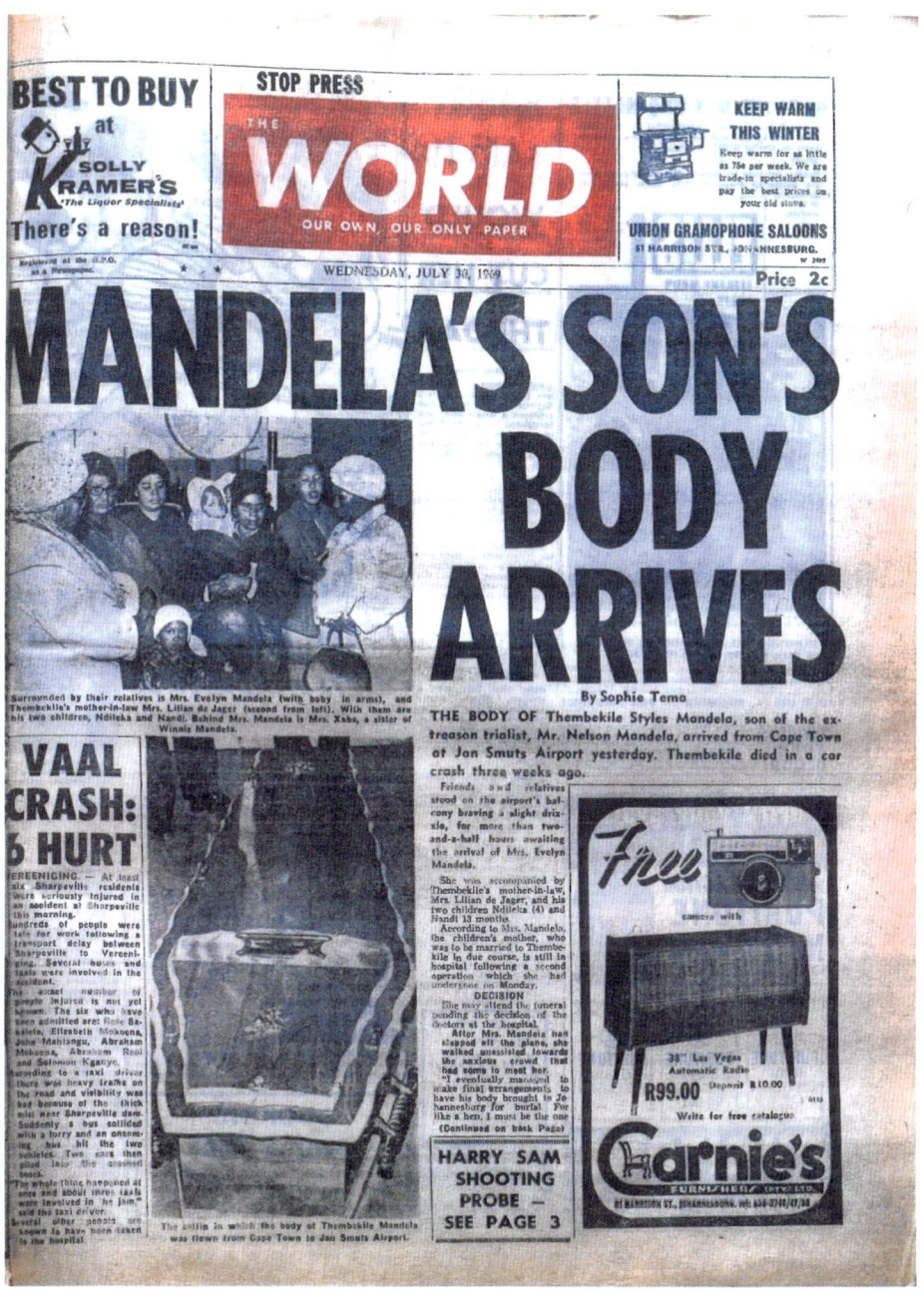

Newspaper clip detailing the arrival of Thembekile's body to Johannesburg

Top left: Tembeka at the age of two

Top right: Pumla at the age of five

Bottom: Tembeka's 11th and Pumla's second birthday party

In Cofimvaba at the age of 18

On the evening of my 40th birthday

Left and right: Tembeka and Hlanganani at preschool in matching outfits

put up with us for long periods. Kaiser Matanzima was one of our regular visitors. He usually came with several men. He was close family and Nelson loved and adored him.'

Chief K.D. Matanzima lived in Qamata, which was pretty close to Cofimvaba.

I vaguely remember all our belongings in the Orlando East house being packed into trucks before we left Johannesburg in June 1972. I guess I was too excited, as this was another adventure for me. We took a train to Queenstown and were picked up by Aunt Lulama, who was Rundu's niece by her older sister, Kate. I remember I was impressed by her, as she was driving a white Cortina.

We arrived in Cofimvaba, a small village town that was to teach me many lessons. The shop Rundu had bought was called Muller Stores, after the owner Mr Muller. She later changed the shop's name to Maliyavuza Store, which roughly translated means 'money is leaking'. It is only now that I understand the name Maliyavuza does not literally mean 'leaking money', rather 'money is flowing'. Maliyavuza was a general dealer store selling anything from groceries to hardware to clothes.

Rundu threw herself into learning how to run a business. She was a community nurse and a midwife and had never run a business before. Aunt Lulama took time to teach her. I'm still amazed to this day by how she managed the switch from being a nurse to a savvy businesswoman. This was in the days when there were very few women who ran businesses. In Cofimvaba, she was the first, followed by Mrs Magaqa. There were naysayers who professed that they wanted to see how long she would be able to hold her own. She held her own and surpassed many a spectator's expectations. She had never done accounting but learnt to balance the books and, in no time, she was good at it.

Rundu was a non-conformist par excellence. When the Watch Tower Bible and Tract Society from Elandsfontein had an article in *Awake!* magazine in the late '70s saying that smoking was harmful, Rundu stopped selling cigarettes at her shop. She even put up a sign saying, 'No Smoking'. She did not care that this would impact on the business, as cigarettes were a big income generator. We were the subject of gossip for a while, but it did not make any difference to her. She made the decision based on principle and in keeping with the tenets of Jehovah's Witnesses. This was my first lesson in non-conformity, and many would follow.

From the time we arrived in Cofimvaba, Rundu became a matriarch who was to shape my life. Life in Cofimvaba followed a certain routine. By the time I started standard five I knew my routine. I would wake up, brush my teeth and sometimes make sour porridge so we could have it before we left for school. After bathing, we would read the morning Bible text. These texts were excerpts of a Bible verse with a theme to set our spiritual focus for the day. After that and a morning prayer, I would have the porridge, or sometimes ProNutro, which I hated. If I woke up late, it would just be prayer and breakfast before I left for school.

School started at 07:45 am and finished at 2 pm. Then there would be afternoon studies from 3 pm until 4 pm. My chores, outside of vacation time, were set around these times. After school was out at 2 pm, I would go home and have lunch quickly. Sometimes I would be required to start the fire so that one of my aunts could get started on dinner. I would then go for afternoon studies. After that, since there was no time for idleness in Rundu's house, I would be required to go to the shop to assist in pricing goods or packing them or manning the cashier register.

The shop closed at 5 pm. Sometimes I would assist Rundu

in counting how much we made from sales, preparing the float for the following day and leaving her behind to balance the books. If it was a Monday, when I left the shop, I would have a bath and, since I did my homework during afternoon study, my cousins and I would prepare for Bible study, which would start promptly at 6 pm. It would end at 7 pm, at which time we had dinner and washed the dishes, making sure there were no leftover soaked pots, as Rundu would wake us up if there were. She believed that dirty dishes and/or soaked pots attracted cockroaches. There couldn't be one dish hanging on the drying rail in the kitchen before we went to bed. To this day, I drive my children nuts with the rule of no dishes in the sink.

There was also a routine for Bible studies, which went something like this:

- Monday – prepare whatever publication for a group Bible study for Tuesday evening
- Tuesday – group Bible study, which was on a rotational basis from one household to another
- Wednesday – prepare for congregational study
- Thursday – congregational study
- Friday – start preparing Watch Tower study for Sunday
- Saturday – street work
- Sunday – Watch Tower discussion and public talk in one of the congregations

Despite this seemingly hectic schedule, I still found time to play. One of the things Rundu taught me was to self-entertain. She greatly disliked the visiting of friends, as she considered them gossipers. She would say, 'You see your friends at school all day long.' Her rationale was that since I saw my friends at school during break, what was there to talk about?

And she thought that once we ran out of things to talk about, we would gossip. As a parent now, I tend to agree. If any of my friends came to see me, she would tell them politely and emphatically that I was busy. I was embarrassed once. I must have been around 13. Landiwe Menera, one of my friends, who's still my friend to this day, came to the shop to buy something. Rundu was behind the shop in her office. After Landiwe finished with her purchases, we ended up chatting at the far end of the shop, as it was not busy. Out of the blue Rundu came out and said, '*Landiwe uNdileka uyasebenza, goduka uyosebenza kokwenu.*' (Landiwe, Ndileka is busy working, go home and work). I was mortified. I was entering puberty; looking and being cool with friends was of paramount importance at this stage of my life. Rundu did not care, as again it was based on principle.

Another example of not conforming happened during the early '80s with the introduction of G-string underwear, which we called *tanga*. Up until that point, we wore full underwear – *nomqondiso* or granny panties, as they are called now. Nandi and my cousin Nobuntu and I went to buy ours at Mr Pambuka's shop. To be honest, I hated these *nomqondisos*. One morning during winter, Rundu decided to do an inspection, again out of the blue. Or was it parental instinct? For some reason, that day I was exempted from the inspection. She called Nandi and Nobuntu and lifted their uniforms to see what underwear they were wearing. Lo and behold they were wearing the *tangas*.

All I heard was, '*Hambani niyokhulula, nizakungena ngumkhuhlane.*' (Go and change, you'll catch a cold). I was in stitches as I waited for them outside.

Rundu was strict. There were times she'd decide that we needed to scrub the floor before going to bed or wake us up early in the morning by sprinkling water over us saying,

Evelyn, my grandmother

'*Vukani, kusile*' (Wake up, it's morning).

Rundu spoilt all of us but she was equally strict. Since she had a vegetable garden where she grew mealies, tomatoes, potatoes, carrots, spinach, peas, you name it, one of my chores was to water the garden. Fortunately, she had a sprinkler but not the electronic ones that you can now put a timer on and voila your garden is watered. This was a manual one that I needed to keep moving from one spot to the next.

So strict was Rundu that one time during school holidays, Nandi and my cousins were tasked with looking after Rundu's cattle. They were required to take them to a different grazing field since the one they used to be taken to was being given a break for it to recover and grow more grass. As the eldest, I was in the shop the whole day. They must have veered off to play and were not paying attention when one of Rundu's favourite heifers got stuck in the mud. Cows in the rural areas are given names, and the name of this heifer was Waqhayisa. It was her favourite since it was her first one, a gift from Chief Daliwonga Matanzima. It had birthed a lot of calves and given us plenty of milk. They came home early, around 5 pm, and Rundu asked them where her heifer was. When they would not fess up she sent them back to get her. Strangely, they went back, perhaps with the hope that they would be able to get her out of the mud. They eventually had to come back and tell Rundu the truth, and they got a serious hiding. Sadly, Waqhayisa had to be put down.

As part of teaching me that I would not always have everything at my command, she would make us walk with her to Esikhobeni for the Sunday public talk and Watch Tower study, or to Mcumngco, despite having a car. This taught me adaptability to any situation I would face.

I used to hate that we were not allowed to do things that

other children were allowed to do, but I'm much better for it. In the early '80s Simon Mabunu Sabela started producing movies like *Inyakanyaka* and *Ikati Elimnyama*. These movies would be screened in our town hall. After the first night of the screening, those who had watched it would rave about it at school. Of course, I wanted to go but knew I could not even bring up the topic with Rundu. I then devised a plan that Lamla Stemela would come and ask her. Lamla was carefully decided upon because I knew Rundu liked his mother, Aunt Nomachule. Now, boys feared Rundu, as she was known for her strictness and religious beliefs. I have to give it to Lamla, because he came. It was a cold winter's evening and although it was only after 5 pm, it was starting to get dark. We were sitting in the kitchen when Lamla knocked. Rundu had a deep, intimidating voice. She greeted Lamla warmly and asked him what she could do for him. He proceeded to tell her he'd come to ask for permission to take me to the movies. She then asked him what the movie was about, and he told her that it was *Ikati Elimnyama*. Her response was, '*Likati Elimnyama lantoni elo? uNdileka akayi apho.*' (What black cat is that? Ndileka is not going there). Lamla left and I was crushed, as I had hoped that she would be manipulated into agreeing.

I eventually had to make peace with the fact that I need not conform in order to make it in life – something that is serving me very well now.

From her I learnt to have a thick skin, a trait I would have to rely on during the difficult phases of my life when I had a household of my own, when the things that happened in my family, although not very different from any other family, would be front-page news. At school I was teased for being at street work. Street work is part of the evangelical work done by Jehovah's Witnesses on the streets on Saturdays. Not only was I teased, but some of the people I approached

Evelyn, my grandmother

to talk and sell magazines to could be quite rude, so this type of evangelical work required that I had a thick skin. Also, they were strangers. It could be quite daunting to be rejected by one person and still approach another stranger to do the same thing, but I learnt to be resilient.

When Rundu bought her first car, a Peugeot 404 van with a canopy, I was thrilled. There was nothing I enjoyed more than visiting her brother in Engcobo and seeing my other Mase cousins. It also allowed Rundu to loosen up and not be so strict. Her elder brother, Sam aka Ntsompoyi, but we called him Coco, was easy going. We sometimes spent weekends in Mkhanzi, where Coco stayed with his wife, uMaTshezi, and their grandchildren. With my cousin Thandi we would be tasked with fetching water from a spring. Mkhanzi had fresh spring water from the mountains. On Sunday we would drive back to Cofimvaba, sitting at the back of the van on a sponge mattress with a blanket. Sometimes I wished the weekends would not end.

Rundu introduced me to a lot of relatives. We met the Matanzimas. I remember the first time we went to Qamata to visit Chief K.D. Matanzima. He had the grandest house I had ever seen back then. We were required to *Khahlela-*praise a chief as a form of greeting. With Chief K.D., we were required to say, '*Ahh! Daliwonga.*' Rundu never did that, and the chief accepted it. This was not an act of defiance but one of the tenets of Jehovah's Witnesses that she could not worship anyone except God. To this day, I don't bow or curtesy to anyone.

I loved visits to Chief K.D. Matanzima's houses. I loved the house in Bolotwa the most, where Mam' Nozuko, one of his wives, lived. It was built on a sprawling farm and she had to drive quite a distance along a small tree-lined road to the house. It was impressive, with the latest furniture in those days.

At no point during my upbringing did I think, oops, I'm a Mandela. She brought me up to be grounded and always keep my feet firmly planted on the ground. She used to say, 'Yes, you may be a Mandela. In the final analysis it is how you carry yourself that people will respect you for, not what your surname is.'

From her I learnt the art of giving, and the art of compassion. Fellow Christian brothers and sisters from our congregation came from poor communities and, because they were doing missionary work, did not always have the means of an income. Rundu would give them groceries from the shop on credit. Some of this credit would not be paid but she never made a fuss about that.

Her midwife skills came in handy in the congregation. She would deliver babies for congregation members in their houses. She was good at it. I don't remember even once a birthing mother having sepsis.

She was an enigma of a woman. When I fell pregnant with Tembela, she never pressured me to marry his father, as was customary in the religion. She reported to the elders that I was pregnant. The elders then came to our house to conduct an inquiry, more like an inquest. They asked questions like where and when we met, where we had sex, how many times, and so on. By the time I fell pregnant I had developed a stubborn personality, so I did not answer most of their questions, as I felt it was none of their business. Suffice to say, I was excommunicated. When a person is excommunicated in the church, no one is supposed to greet or talk to them. When I got excommunicated, I wondered how this would pan out, as Rundu and I lived in the same house. I don't think the elders thought this one through. After that excommunication, I never went back to the congregation nor lived my life according to their tenets.

In fact, I had started questioning the tenets of the church once I started boarding school, when I was 15 years old. I got exposed to the Methodist Church and other charismatic churches. My strict upbringing in a Jehovah's Witness household made me rebel against religion for the longest time. I vowed I would never do it to my children. This is a decision I regret in retrospect. As a parent, I now know that although children may veer from the way they were brought up, they will more often than not return to it.

However, some things that are taught to you from an early age never leave you. They become part of your DNA. There are still a lot of things that I do that make me feel like God is sitting there and judging me, like having sex outside of marriage. This was drilled into my head. To this day, I don't donate blood because I was raised a Jehovah's Witness. The church holds this belief about blood donation because of various Bible texts, namely Deutoronomy chapter 12 verse 23, Leveticus chapter 17 verses 10 and 11 and Acts chapter 15 verse 29. From these texts, Jehovah's Witnesses believe blood represents life and is sacred to God and therefore donating blood promotes disobedience to God and accepting blood is tantamount to cannibalism. I also don't believe there is a hell. I don't believe in being bewitched. Rundu scoffed at the very idea of witchcraft. She did believe that there are demons that were cast out of heaven, though.

Rundu also taught me to be generous. I grew up having a lot of clothes. Ouma spoilt me rotten with the latest designer clothes. Every time I went to Cape Town to visit Granddad, I came back with a suitcase full of clothes. Some of these clothes I never got to wear, as I spent most of my time at boarding school. She encouraged me to give away clothes I no longer wanted, which I did.

Cofimvaba was a beautiful community that taught all

of us how to live together in harmony. There was no class distinction and we were brought up to respect all adults. This was a community where an adult could reprimand you, irrespective of whether they were your parent or not, and you would listen.

Around the time I started my midwifery course, Uncle Kgatho relocated to Cofimvaba to live with us. After his arrival, Rundu eased off her strictness but, before then, even though I had started working, Rundu maintained it. In Cofimvaba, around Christmas or New Year, youngsters would go to Port St Johns for picnics. I never even bothered to ask Rundu, as I knew what her response would be, but when Uncle Kgatho joined us, I spoke to him and he was the one to tell Rundu she had to let me go.

After I completed my training as a midwife in July 1989, I went on a joyride with my cousin sis Tumeka Matanzima to the anger of both Rundu and Aunt Maki. Upon my return, Aunt Maki and her husband, Uncle Isaac, drove me to Durban to live with Mom, and I started working at St Aidan's ICU. I also took my son, Tembela, with me. Up until then, he had been staying with his paternal grandparents who were in Cofimvaba. I would visit Rundu in Cofimvaba from time to time.

I saw Rundu regularly again when I quit bedside nursing and joined the pharmaceutical industry in 1995. My work as a medical rep required me to go on field trips to the Eastern Cape and Swaziland. Whenever I did the Eastern Cape field trip, I made sure I went to see Rundu. I would see her on a much more frequent basis after I relocated to Johannesburg in 2000. By then Rundu had started ailing and had to move to Johannesburg, where she stayed with Aunt Maki. Although old age was beginning to take its toll on her – she had diabetes and chest problems – she was still beautiful, and her faith never wavered.

After she turned 82, she was hospitalised at Milpark Hospital in the high care unit with chest problems. I remember the day vividly. Aunt Maki called to tell me she had been admitted and that it did not look good. The date was 27 April 2004. Since it was a public holiday, I told Aunt Maki I would come to visit her the next day, as I was getting my hair done. True to my promise, I went to visit her the next day. Although she did not look good, I did not expect her to die two days later.

In 2004, I had started doing my MBA through correspondence with the University of KwaZulu-Natal. Once every two months, a lecturer would come up to Johannesburg and hold block classes. I was attending one of these classes on 29 April 2004 when I received a call from my cousin Thandi Mase, telling me Rundu was not doing well and she looked confused. I dropped everything I was doing and drove straight to Milpark. When I arrived, I took one look at her and knew it was the beginning of the end. I called Aunt Maki to alert her after chatting to one of her physicians to confirm my suspicions.

They then moved her to a private ward, as she had been in a semi-private ward. That night, Thandi decided to stay over at the hospital to keep her company. 30 April was a Friday. I decided that I was going to be the one that slept over that night and after visiting hours I went home and changed into a tracksuit so I could be comfortable. I went back to the hospital around 8 pm. Uncle Kgatho left Nandi, Tukwini and me with her to go home. It must have been 15 minutes after he left that Rundu became restless. She had oxygen prongs, which she started pulling out. I put them back and asked her not to take them out as they were helping her breathe. All she said to me was, 'It's time.' No sooner had she said that, Mandla came into the ward. He could not come earlier, as he was writing exams at Rhodes University. I asked her if she could see Mandla, to which she said yes. After that she asked us to gather around her bed. We did. She uttered this prayer: '*Thixo ndiwunikela kuwe umphefumlo wam*' (God, I give my soul to you) and then she started gasping, at which point I ran out quickly to call the night nurse to note the time of death.

Rundu had a huge content smile on her face when she took her last breath. It had always been her wish to die surrounded by her grandchildren and on that night all the firstborns from all three of her children were in the room with her when it happened. She had got her wish. I called Uncle Kgatho to tell him to make his way back to the hospital. Our family descended on Milpark that night to await the undertaker who would take her to Kopano Mortuaries.

She was buried the following Saturday at Westpark Cemetery and her service was conducted by Jehovah's Witnesses.

I am eternally grateful to God for having the grace and favour of allowing me to be moulded by her. From Rundu I learnt how to be grounded, hardworking, graceful, have dignity and above all not to carry my name on my sleeve like a badge, but to work hard to be worthy of it.

Chapter 7

Ouma, my maternal grandmother

I HAVE BEEN BLESSED IN MY LIFE because I had two great matriarchs shaping and moulding me. Ouma, as we all called my maternal grandmother, was a formidable woman. Although I only saw her during holidays, she had an immense impact on me. It seems I have always been surrounded by women who refused to conform to the positions they were relegated to.

Ouma stayed in Retreat, Cape Town, on 7th Avenue, a predominantly coloured area that would at times be raided by police to see if there were black people staying there. I would have to speak Kaapse Afrikaans when I was in Retreat, which I hated.

Ouma, like Rundu, also had an enormous property. This was the first place where I saw a television set. Ouma had a small set and we would walk from Mom's *pondotjie* (a house made of corrugated iron sheets) to watch TV there. Those days, SAUK/SABC started their programmes at 5 pm, I think. I'm talking way back in the early '80s. We would watch *Liewe Heksie, Shanana, Eight is Enough* and so on.

When she built a bigger house on the same property and had a bigger TV, she would almost force us all to watch tennis with her. As time went by, I grew to love watching tennis. We would watch the likes of Björn Borg and Martina Navratilova.

She also had a soft-top convertible Tempest and I loved driving in it with her. While in Cofimvaba I was learning fundamental skills from Rundu, Ouma was putting me through 'finishing' school. She would tell me a girl should not slouch when she walks, and she always has to hold her tummy in. This was to be one of my first lessons from her.

When I turned 16 and went to visit Granddad, she noticed that my boobs were big and needed support. She did not hesitate to take me to a bra shop to buy me properly fitting bras. Both Rundu and Mom had thought it was still early to wear a bra. Guess what, Ouma was right – I had very big boobs in my teen years and when we went for the fitting the sales lady told Ouma that if I had delayed being fitted with a correct bra, I would have developed upper back problems. At 16 I wore a 34DDD cup, which was too big for my small frame then.

In 1983, when I visited Ouma, I asked her if she could take me to get my hair permed. We found a salon in Diep River where they could do a perm on coarse hair. I had seen Yoliswa Balfour back in Cofimvaba with a beautiful perm and had longed to have my hair permed but knew it was pointless asking Rundu.

Ouma loved clothes and she dressed extremely well. She taught me a lot of things about fashion. She would be the first person to teach me that if you were overweight you could not wear horizontal stripes, as they would make you look bigger. She also made sure I was always dressed in the latest fashion. She would take me to Stuttafords to buy clothes, from Jodarche jeans to Escada jackets. Not that I knew what these brand names meant then. I only started learning about fashion brands when I went to Nyanga High School, where there were other students interested in fashion.

Life in Retreat could be confusing at times, but thanks to Rundu I never lost my identity. Retreat was a coloureds-only suburb and it was illegal for people classified as black to live in the area. Because of this, Ouma used to tell us to always wear hats, especially if she saw a police van approaching. This was to cover our *'krouse hare'* – coarse hair. I hated this with a passion.

Ouma showed me to a life that I was not exposed to by Rundu and in Cofimvaba. This was a life of high fashion, a life of watching competitive sports like tennis, a life of testing boundaries with authority.

Sadly, Ouma succumbed to a brain tumour and died at home in Retreat in 1993. After her funeral, I never visited Retreat again, as I felt it would never be the same without her.

From these two matriarchs, I learnt how to be a non-conformist. They both pushed boundaries. They both owned businesses and vast properties without husbands. While Rundu was pushing boundaries by being a savvy and shrewd businesswoman in the early '70s, Ouma was amassing vast property in a coloureds-only area.

Looking back at my life and early childhood now, I can see how I learnt to strike a balance between these two lifestyles.

Part Three

Chapter 8

Motherhood

IF ANYONE TOLD ME THAT I WOULD be a mother by the time I turned 19, I would have thought they were crazy.

I say this for many reasons. The top reason is that I was brought up in a very strict religious Jehovah's Witness household where premarital sex was taboo and against biblical practices. My pregnancy was confirmed by a doctor in Cape Town, where Ouma took me, after she became suspicious of how my body had changed. I remember her calling Mom in Durban and telling her. I don't remember what Mom said to her, but I do know that she was displeased with me and the situation. Ouma had wanted me to stay with her, but Rundu would not have it.

I then returned to Cofimvaba. Two weeks after my return, a call from Durban came and my stepfather, Daddy Phineas, was on the phone. He wanted me to come and stay in Durban for the duration of my pregnancy and I refused. He then gave me an ultimatum: I had to return to Durban or never set foot there again. For reasons I'd rather not talk about, I was dead set against going to Durban, so I stayed in Cofimvaba. I was angry with my mother, as I felt she was again refusing to talk to me as she had done when she married my stepfather. Rundu was in Queenstown when this call came through and when I told her of the conversation, she hit the roof.

During the entire duration of my pregnancy, I did not speak to my mother nor did I see her until Daddy Phineas died in 1986 and I had to go to his funeral in Nongoma. My mother only met my son, Tembela, when he was a year old.

Back to my pregnancy in Cofimvaba. Both Rundu and Ouma gave all the love and care they could give me. Rundu made sure I went to all my antenatal classes and she bought me all the prenatal vitamins I needed. Since she was a midwife, I thought she would birth my son as I had seen her birthing many children in our congregation.

When I was about 38 weeks pregnant, she sent me to stay with Uncle Nkululeko Mase and his wife, who lived in Mthatha, as she wanted me to give birth at St Mary's Hospital.

Tembela Thembisile Mandela was born around 6 am on 27 November 1984, weighing 2.8 kg. I had never known love like the love I felt for my son. He was delivered normally but the nurses had to perform an episiotomy. After my stitches were healed, I returned to Cofimvaba with my son.

Ouma sent two very large boxes full of baby clothes, all from Stuttafords. Rundu bought me baby clothes too.

Tembela was a colicky baby and had me at my wit's end when we returned to Cofimvaba. He only settled when Rundu got him colic medication from Magers, a pharmacy in Queenstown.

I was determined to take care of Tembela myself but when he was five months old I had to leave him behind with his paternal grandmother, who was a nurse, to start my own training as a professional nurse. Rundu was already over the age of 60 at this point and it did not seem fair to have her take care of a five-month-old baby. This is a decision I would regret years later. I feel that I missed out on the most crucial time in my child's life – early childhood.

Although I would see him almost every time I was off duty, I missed all his milestones. I missed seeing him cut his first teeth, I missed the first time he crawled, his first step, his first word.

The day I left him to start training is still a vivid memory. The previous night I had spent packing both his and my clothes, as his paternal grandmother was to pick him up the next day. He was still being breastfed and only drank breast milk. I spent the night crying, worried sick, not knowing whether he would take to formula. Tearing myself from him as I left him sitting on his chair in Rundu's kitchen was the hardest thing I had to do.

By the time Rundu and I reached Glen Grey Hospital in Lady Frere, my breasts were engorged and leaking. I was advised not to express and one of the matrons gave me tablets to dry up the milk.

Tembela stayed with his paternal grandparents until I completed my midwifery training in 1989. When I started working at St Aidan's Hospital, I went to get him to come and live with my mother and me in Durban. He was now four years old and I wanted him to start kindergarten. His grandmother and I had an agreement that when I completed my training, I was to take over his upbringing.

This was extremely hard on him. Although he knew who I was, he had grown attached to his paternal family. He cried a lot when we left them for Durban. It tore my heart to do this to him, but I had to do what I felt was best for him. Durban offered better schools than Cofimvaba and I wanted him with me.

I immediately took him to start kindergarten at a school Mom and my aunt Beryl Sisulu had found for him in Sydenham. Slowly, he started adjusting to Durban and was soon joined by my nephew Hlanganani, my sister Nandi's son, who was around 3 years old.

Life settled a bit for him and the very same year, in December, I allowed him to visit his paternal family in Cofimvaba. When it was time for him to come back, he did not want to, but I insisted that he be brought back. I'm told he cried for half of the journey back to Durban. Not only was he crying, his aunts were also crying. This really got me annoyed, as I felt that it was not as if he wouldn't come back to visit and they were making the situation unnecessarily hard, especially for him. I decided then that if that was going to be the case every time he visited, he'd rather not visit at all.

I have often wondered about this decision, but I guess as a mother I had to make it, as I felt it was best for him.

When Tembela arrived back in Durban he was next to hysterical, to an extent that I almost allowed him to go back. His screams tore at my heart. Mom gave me the strength to push on. Tembela was now five years old, and he had become very withdrawn, so much so that I had to take him to see a child psychologist, who also felt that it was best for him not to visit Cofimvaba until he had adjusted.

By the time Tembela reached grade five it became clear that he had learning difficulties. I took him to a remedial school called Phoenix Primary School, where he started thriving and excelled in soccer.

In 1990, after Granddad insisted that I go back to study, I started my degree in nursing at MEDUNSA. He got me a bursary with the South African Council of Churches. This was not a full bursary and I had to rely on my mom giving me money to supplement my needs.

Since I had left Tembela with her to study, she also had to take care of him and, as such, the pocket money she sent me was not sufficient. This was quite frustrating as I was used to earning a good income as an ICU nurse.

When Granddad was released on 11 February 1990, I was hopeful that I would not battle with money. Again, I was wrong. It was difficult to have free access to him after his release. Even when I did manage to see him, I could not have a private moment with him. He was constantly surrounded by people. When I did manage to have a few moments with him and told him about my plight, he would refer me to other people.

After a couple of times trying to sort out my monetary problems and failing, I turned to Rundu to assist me and she did whenever she could. By the time I had to sit for the final exam for my degree, I was fed up and decided I was not going back to MEDUNSA. I did not tell Granddad I had quit. I simply asked Aunt Fatima to get me my job at St Aidan's Hospital back. She was the one who had got me the job the first time.

I settled back into my job and taking care of Tembela. His father was no longer in the picture, nor were his grandparents. In fact, we had broken up when Tembela was about four years old.

I started a new relationship in January 1991 and in February 1993 I fell pregnant with Pumla. I was 28. Unlike my first pregnancy, which was unplanned and a shock, this one was planned. From the beginning of the pregnancy, I wanted to do things differently. I was working and earning a good income again. I gave birth to my daughter and named her Pumla, both after my Aunt Makaziwe, whose middle name is Pumla, and because my womb would now rest.

I had always wanted and planned to only have two

children, married or not. I knew with the utmost clarity that my womb would definitely rest. I remember telling my mother that I would have my second child before I turned 30, as I would not want to stretch both my stomach and my body after 30 because it is difficult to get your body back into shape after that. Writing this book now, I am astounded by my vanity and clarity. In retrospect, it's a reminder that whatever you declare verbally or mentally does come to pass, which I know now.

From the time Pumla was born, I knew we would be friends. She did not have colic, as her brother did. I would stare at my baby girl for hours as she slept. When she was three months old, I went back to work. Tembela and Hlanganani doted on Pumla, but it was with Hlanganani that she bonded most, as they are more alike in character.

When Pumla was about seven months old, Granddad bought Nandi and me a house in Westville and we ventured out on our own with our children. Later on, Granddad bought me my own house in Pinetown in 1997.

Around the time Pumla was about five years old, in 1998, I moved to Johannesburg for a job with Prime Cure Clinics. This was a primary healthcare group of clinics. I had started working for Prime Cure in 1997 and this was a promotion to work in their marketing department, which was based in Centurion.

Since the transfer was mid-year, I left both Tembela and Pumla with my housekeeper and would drive to Durban every fortnight. I put the house in Pinetown up for sale and moved with the children to Johannesburg in December 1999. I bought another house in Randpark Ridge.

I found schools for both my children, Tembela at Northcliff High and Pumla at Randpark Primary. Before long, our lives settled into a routine of me dropping off both of them at their respective schools and then driving off to my job in Centurion.

Tembela's first love was soccer and he was highly frustrated that Northcliff did not offer soccer. Model C schools at the time only offered rugby. I had to find a place for him at the Randburg Football Club. This was challenging, as their matches were sometimes late at night.

Pumla settled nicely at Randpark Primary and by the time she was in Grade Five she started ballet classes. A year later she pestered me to enrol her in an Irish dancing class, which most of her ballet friends were also doing. She was very good at both but mostly at Irish dancing. She won many competitions.

As a single mother, both my children kept me busy. Between athletics days, soccer, ballet and Irish dancing classes, my hands were full. At times I would hardly have a weekend to myself, as I would have to take Pumla to her competitions.

Being a soccer mom was extremely challenging. I had to learn how to sew satin ribbons to shoes for ballet, and watch soccer matches late at night, which was often difficult, as I had to supervise homework too.

Sadly, Tembela's soccer days came to an abrupt end after he sustained a knee injury. He tore his PCL – posterior cruciate ligament, one of the ligaments responsible for stabilising the knee joint. He had to go for extended physiotherapy and his therapist advised that he be extremely careful, as another injury would warrant him having a knee replacement later in his life. Although he stopped competitive soccer after that, that knee still bothers him to this day.

Pumla was progressing well at school and by the time she was starting high school at St Mary's, Tembela had finished high school and was studying music production at the Soul Candy Institute of Music.

It was Mama Graça Machel who advised me to look for a private school for Pumla. She told me she saw great potential in both Pumla and Zeni Jnr (Aunt Zindzi's eldest daughter).

I remember that St Mary's was the only school I applied to for her. As it is customary for all new applicants, parents are asked to come to orientation before their children are admitted. I struck up a friendship with another mother by the name of Nikky Mogorosi. As we were being taken around the school, we overheard other parents talking among themselves about how the following weekend they were going to a different school for orientation.

I remember Nikky looking at me and asking if I'd applied to any other school, to which I told her St Mary's was it.

We both left worried in case our daughters were not admitted and both concerned that if they were not, we were going to battle finding them another good school, as applications closed early.

It turned out we need not have worried, for, by God's grace, they were both admitted.

Since Tembela was now at a tertiary institution, I did not have to worry that much about him and could focus almost entirely on Pumla's high school education. Dropping Pumla at school before work could be challenging. The school did not have enough parking and there was a huge sign saying that parents must drop off their children and not park so as not to cause a jam in the parking lot. Of course, there were parents who did not heed this sign and would have a big fat chat in the parking lot. I used to call them the 'Parking Lot Brigade'.

When Pumla was in Grade 10, she took drama lessons. Sometimes, the students attended drama sessions at Wits, which ended late most of the time, often after 10 pm, which I found quite annoying. Pumla would still have a lot of homework to go through. I don't know how she managed, but she did.

Another one of my pet peeves was parents' night. Again, you'd find parents who would hog teachers. I remember during one of these evenings, I had been waiting my turn for one of Pumla's teachers and overheard a parent whose child had received 95% in the subject asking the teacher what she thought the problem was. Seriously?! I could see the teacher wanted to roll her eyes.

When Pumla started high school, she decided to quit ballet, something she now regrets. She had stopped Irish dancing in her last year at primary school too.

While I had to push Tembela with his schoolwork, I never had to do that with Pumla. She has always been self-driven, and her group of friends were the same.

Before I knew it, it was time for her matric dance. Where did the time go?

Girls always have a group of friends they plan their matric dance pre-drinks with. It was no different with her and her friends. I had maintained a close and friendly relationship with Pumla. She could ask me about anything.

Their pre-drinks rendezvous was to be held at a parent's house in Atholl-Oaklands. Pumla was now 18 years old. Of course, I had bought and chilled a bottle of Champagne to toast the girls before they left for the dance, but upon arriving at the house the other parents were dead set against their children drinking alcohol. I honestly did not see what the big fuss was, as I had introduced Pumla to Champagne when she turned 16. In my household, alcohol could be taken with food. I felt it was important for me to do that so I could see how she behaved after a glass of alcohol and monitor it in a controlled environment.

I had been brought up in an extremely strict environment

and had gone crazy when I was introduced to alcohol when I started nursing studies. I did not want my daughter to have the same wild experience without knowing and learning for herself what her limits were. I was determined that if she was to drink alcohol, I was going to be the one introducing her to it.

As I was about to divulge this to the parents, my sister, Zinhle, gave me a look that said don't you dare. A couple of us parents had hired a stretch limo for the girls. As they were about to leave, I took the bottle of Champagne I had brought and put it in Pumla's bag, where she had put a change of clothing she'd wear for the after party.

As soon as they left, one of the parents remembered that the limos always put complimentary Champagne in the car. She then decided to quickly drive to the school and retrieve it. I knew these children had most probably popped the Champagne and were drinking it. I quickly called Pumla to ask them if they had opened the Champagne and she told me they were indeed drinking it. I could hear the excitement in the background. When I told her one of the mothers was on her way to retrieve the bottle, they were so panicked that I told them to relax and have the Champagne I had put in Pumla's bag.

After she passed her matric with flying colours, she decided to take a gap year. There were some family members that were opposed to this idea, but because I had come to understand Pumla, I allowed her to have the gap year. If she needed this, I was going to allow her to have it.

Nikky's daughter, Tsholofelo, was also taking a gap year and she and Pumla had become very close friends during their time at St Mary's. Nikky suggested that instead of just sitting at home and idling, they should do something meaningful with the gap year. Nikky is from Marapyane in

Mpumalanga and she had a house there. They went over and for a small stipend they taught English to Grade 10 learners at Marapyane High school.

This experience made Pumla mature and appreciate things she had taken for granted for a long time. It also gave her time to decide what she wanted to do next. During the gap year, she applied to the University of Cape Town for a degree in social sciences. Although this was emotionally difficult for me, as she'd never been on her own and this far away her entire life, I had to let go. Since I had been opposed to her to being at boarding school, I had to allow her to go to UCT and venture out on her own.

She got accepted at UCT and, early in February 2013, I accompanied her there to help her settle. While she was busy with registration, I helped set up her room with all the basic necessities because I knew from my experience of going to MEDUNSA, and not having enough money, how important it was for me to do that.

After years of being away from Cape Town and not visiting it, I found it a bit slow. After four days, I couldn't wait to get back to Johannesburg.

What I did not expect was the loneliness I felt when I came back home. I went to Pumla's room and the emptiness hit me like blunt-force trauma. Yes, Pumla had been away from home to spend weekends with friends, but this was different. It would be a while before I saw her again. I was worried by a lot of things, but I had to trust that the values I had imparted on her would serve her well.

At least my 'nest' was not entirely empty, as Tembela was still at home, trying his hand at rap music. He writes beautiful poetry, which I have tried many a time to steer him towards, to no avail. I guess our role as parents is to give guidance and support to our children and let them choose their own paths.

I have had to finally accept that both my children will walk their own journeys and choose their own paths.

When Granddad took seriously ill during Pumla's first year at varsity, I was extremely worried it would disrupt her balance as she was trying to find her feet, to an extent that I would water down his condition whenever she called to ask. It also did not help that the media would broadcast his bouts of hospitalisation. I had to accept that being part of my family came with certain challenges and, although I had taught them this from an early age, I wished at times they could be spared the constant barrage of information about Granddad's illness. I found myself praying that, when the inevitable came, she would be on vacation to allow her mourning time and time to process things before she went back to varsity. As I always maintain, if you say something to the universe enough, it will oblige you. Granddad transitioned from this world during her December vacation.

The following year she continued with her studies at UCT. Then came the #FeesMustFall campaign, which began on Monday, 12 October 2015. At that point, Pumla was in the last year of her degree. As much as I saw images of the campaign and how brutal the police were towards our children, I was still a bit removed from the enormity of it, until Pumla called me to tell me she and her friends were joining the march to Parliament.

This both surprised me and made me proud as her mother. I was proud because, although she was not really affected by the fluctuating fees, as Granddad had set up an education fund, she was marching out of principle.

That pride soon turned to fear. As soon as she told me she was part of the march, I rushed home so I could watch it live. When the police threw teargas and started shooting with rubber bullets at students who were kneeling, I watched in horror. I also watched the minister of higher education and training tell the police to shoot at unarmed students. I went ballistic. I was literally frantic. I called every person I knew but some were inside Parliament and were not answering their phones.

When the son of Rev. Frank Chikane got arrested, I went even more ballistic. How could I accept that police were arresting students who just wanted to hand over a petition? Had our politicians gone nuts? How could the child of a struggle veteran like Frank Chikane be charged with treason?

To top it all, after watching how violent that march became, I could not get hold of Pumla. After about an hour she called me back, panting as if she had been running, and told me she was okay. What she did not tell me at the time was that she was part of the students who got temporarily closed behind the gates of Parliament and the police were refusing to let them go.

This incident and the whole #FeesMustFall period really affected Pumla and South African students as a whole. Pumla became slightly depressed after that, partly because of the trauma she had experienced and because her degree became extended by a whole six months. Their exams had to be deferred. I can't begin to imagine how this deferment affected parents who were paying out of their pocket.

Due to the deferment, she completed her undergraduate degree in June 2016. Shortly after she came home, she had more surprising news. I was in the office the day she broke the news of her pregnancy. She had called me to ask when I would be home, as she wanted to tell me something. Due to my impatience at times, I asked her to tell me right there and then. She blurted out, 'Mom, I'm pregnant.' I said, 'Okay, we'll talk when I get home.'

I thank God she was with one of her more mature friends

when she made the call, as I could tell she was nervous. I did not know how to process this. All I knew was that she had just completed her undergraduate degree and for that I was grateful. From the time I turned 50 the previous year, I'd been ready for grandchildren.

Now I had to see to it that the traditional ritual of *Ukubika Isisu*, a tradition where the girl's family goes and informs the boy's family of the pregnancy, was performed. I called my cousin Mandla to ask him what our Thembu traditional procedure was. With both my pregnancies, 'damages' were paid. This call to Mandla was made after Dabs, Aunt Maki, and all my siblings were informed. In September 2016, Pumla and I travelled to Qunu for this ritual to be attended to. We travelled to the father of the child's family in East London and they were 'fined'.

It was then back to Johannesburg. Pumla's pregnancy went smoothly, thank God. Since she is a petite girl, her obstetrician-gynae recommended a Caesarean and, as a midwife, I agreed. Nabeela was born on 27 February 2017, weighing 3.5 kgs. I was really blessed to be with both Pumla and Nabeela's father inside the theatre when she was born.

We named her Nabeela Thokozile, after my mother. I can't explain the joy I felt when I held my first grandchild in my arms. The love I had, still have, that grows daily, is immeasurable. I don't know what it is about grandchildren that makes your heart swell with so much love it threatens to choke you.

Nabeela, or Nana as we call her, is truly blessed. She is the first great-great-grandchild, born of the first great-granddaughter, whose mother was the first grandchild, born of the firstborn of the first wife of Nelson Rolihlahla Mandela. That makes her first, five times, an honour and great responsibility.

Motherhood

Nabeela is teaching me new things about myself and I have been privileged to watch her grow and witness every one of her milestones, something I sometimes missed with my own children.

Motherhood has taught me many lessons. Chief among them are the following:

- To be more patient: This applied especially with Tembela as he had learning difficulties.
- To be less of a control freak: Life in general has taught me that I am never in control. There is a higher being that is in charge. I can't control my children's choices. I have had to allow both of them to make their own choices in life. My duty is just to guide them.
- To accept different views: For instance, I did not entirely agree with the stance taken by students regarding the Cecil Rhodes statue. My stance was that these statues refer to a different time in our history and wiping away history does not get us anywhere, as we are bound to repeat it. I asked Pumla, who was at UCT at the time, what would happen perhaps 100 years from now to all the statues of the liberation movement figures, when perhaps South Africa has a different regime? Her response was to highlight what the Rhodes statue represents, an institution that refuses to transform. This was something I was not aware of and my daughter became my teacher.
- How challenging single parenthood can be: In fact, single parenthood has both an upside and downside to it. The upside of it, in my experience, is that you have a single centre of command. You have no opposing side to the way you run things, especially discipline. This I found to be a blessing. The downside outweighs the upside, though. The downside I've experienced

has been the fact that, as a single parent, there is no downtime for you. You can't check out, as there is no husband to take over. This has been compounded by urbanisation where the extended family structures hardly exist anymore. In the olden days, this extended family structure assisted in single parenthood. It is fact that the term 'single parenthood' didn't make sense in the African context. Another fact is that children from single parent households do not have a balanced view of life, as they have only seen life from the vantage point of whichever parent brought them up, mother or father. To this day, if I had to do things all over again, I am not sure if I would choose differently.

- You stop doing as you please, as you have a responsibility towards your children: The first teacher of a child is the parent and in the case of my children, it was me. It was important for me to impart on them and teach them what Rundu, Ouma and my mother taught me.

As challenging as motherhood has been at times, especially as a single parent, I wouldn't have it any other way. My children have brought me so much joy and have returned me to sanity when things have been extremely tough for me, to the point of contemplating suicide. They have brought me back from the point of destruction. No one, not even my sisters, could ever be the mother I am to my children. I guess the ONLY reason I have never committed suicide when things got unbearably tough for me was the thought that no one could raise them my way, and my way is best.

The greatest regret I have as a mother is that I short-changed Tembela. The woman I am now has seen first-hand what growing up without a father or father figure can do to boys. I can be quite overbearing as a mother, owing to being raised by strong matriarchs. That can't have been easy for Tembela, but I am grateful to God that he is coming into his own and finding his niche in life.

For Pumla I guess it was easy; all she had to do was look at me and emulate me.

If I had to do things all over again, I would never raise children on my own.

Chapter 9

The importance of education

FROM AN EARLY AGE, IT WAS drummed into my head how important education is, and I've come to believe so. This was not only scholastically, but also in broadening my mind with a lot of other things. I believe education is not only about what you learn in a classroom, but general knowledge as well.

At primary school I was extremely good at comprehension. This skill I learnt solely at home, growing up in a Jehovah's Witness household. I mentioned earlier how we would do Bible and Watchtower study. Watchtower study is no more than reading a piece and extracting the salient points in each paragraph. This taught me comprehension. The *Watchtower* magazine is set out in different sections and all of them have themes. Two or three of these 'themed' sections are set out in comprehension style with questions for each paragraph. Doing this at home sharpened my skills of extracting salient points in any comprehension at school. This skill served me extremely well when I later went to study nursing.

There was also the *Awake!* magazine, which had well-researched medical articles. Looking back now, I think that is what drew me to nursing. That and the fact that our parents are our first role models. Growing up and seeing Rundu dressed up in a nursing uniform automatically pushed me to nursing, even if it was subliminal at the time.

The importance of education was also drummed into my head by my granddad. Every letter he wrote to me was about education. A few years ago, I discovered that Granddad had done the same thing with my parents, especially my mother, after Dad died.

In one of the letters he wrote to my mother a few months after Dad died, he advises her to go back to school, as this will allow her the independence of taking care of my sister and me.

In another letter to Mom, dated 24 March 1970, referring to Uncle Kgatho, he says:

> *During his last visit Kgatho told me he would leave for Fort Hare on February 14. I have received no confirmation of this and I have accordingly not written to him. Please advise me whether he is at college. I was happy to hear that Beryl (Sisulu) has started at Groote Schuur and wish her real success in her studies.*

As you can see, he was happy with Aunt Beryl and not so happy with Uncle Kgatho, to the point of not writing to him. I remember facing the same wrath from him after he learnt that I had quit MEDUNSA.

Education has been important to me for these reasons:
- It has broadened my horizons by expanding my knowledge of my environment and the world around me.
- It has helped me build informed opinions about things

in life I have not necessarily experienced.

In general, I feel, education gives us a perspective of looking at life. Many debate whether education is the only thing that gives us knowledge, while some say education is the process of gaining information about the surrounding world and knowledge is something very different. Others argue that information cannot be converted into knowledge without education, as education makes us capable of interpreting things.

I feel this is true to an extent. I have gathered many life lessons, like indigenous African knowledge, that I did not learn in a classroom. These lessons are, for instance, how I spoke to my elders and how I respected every elder irrespective of whether they were my parent or not.

It is only recently that I have started appreciating the African indigenous knowledge system, specifically when it comes to the treatment of illness. This is something I saw in my childhood, and it is something I want to impart to Nabeela, as I have sort of missed the boat with Pumla.

In Cofimvaba, as with the whole of Eastern Cape, aloe grows wild. Rundu would cut aloe and bottle it for us to drink for ailments like stomach aches, headaches and period pains. This concoction worked. When we had flus or colds, she would boil gum tree leaves and give us the liquid to steam with. The following day, I would be right as rain, without any of the side effects modern medicine would predispose me to.

I also believe that legalising marijuana for medicinal use at home is the best thing our country has done. I don't understand how an organic herb can have worse side effects than pharmaceutical medicines, but that's a debate for another day.

Back to the importance of education, both inside and outside of the classroom and in particular regarding my nursing education. Nursing exposed me to a whole new world. I fell in love with my work. In my first year, I learnt about anatomy, but nothing interested me like physiology, which I learnt in my second year.

Two systems fascinated me the most, the circulatory and nervous systems. Prior to studying nursing, I didn't know the heart was controlled by an electromagnetic mechanism that no human being can regenerate. The very human conception can never be replicated outside a sperm and an ovum.

Now when you talk about the nervous system, you talk of the most impressive supercomputer known to mankind. The neurons that crisscross our bodies (cells responsible for sensory input from the external world, for sending motor commands to our muscles and for transforming and relaying electrical signals) are complicated and they work without our command or will.

I think if I had gone ahead with my studies, I would have proceeded to study medicine and become a cardiothoracic or neuro surgeon.

I loved what I was learning and putting into practice. I cruised through my general nursing training, and then came midwifery. If I found general nursing to be fascinating, midwifery was exceptional. From the time of conception to the delivery room, midwifery offered me more wonder. These were the days when we listened to the foetus's heartbeat with a fetoscope. I doubt if nurses training today will know what that is. At St Barnabas, where I did my midwifery training, we were even taught how to deliver breach babies.

Before I knew it, my training was over and I went to work at the ICU at St Aidan's Hospital, a semi-private hospital in Durban.

The difference between private and public hospitals was a culture shock for me. Not only was the patient/nurse ratio one to one, at least in the ICU where I worked, you also had to record everything you used for the patient, from the syringe, to the needle, to the cotton wool swabs. You see, everything you used for the patient was charged to the patient. The wastage between private and public hospitals is incomparable.

A skill I learnt while working in the ICU was to be extremely observant, something that has stayed with me to date. In ICU, I could not afford to miss the slightest change with a patient, as that was the difference between life and death.

At St Aidan's I was also sent for training as a renal nurse at King Edward VIII Hospital. While I enjoyed the training, it was not as exciting to me as the other fields of nursing, but it was a feather in my cap and more knowledge.

As much as I loved nursing, I could not take night duty. In the end, it is night duty that ended my love affair with nursing and pushed me to seek out new opportunities. When I left nursing, I joined the pharmaceutical industry first with Sandoz then Scherag. Before entering the industry, I used to think that a pharmaceutical rep was a glorified salesperson who marketed whatever drugs were on her list. I was wrong. Pharmaceutical reps are well-trained individuals who are taught the pharmacokinetics and pharmacodynamics of medicine.

After leaving the pharmaceutical industry, I joined a pathology lab and finally the medical aid industry, thus going almost full circle in the health industry field.

As much as I gained knowledge during my life through education and in the different industries, I cannot diminish the life lessons I also learnt, in particular regarding indigenous knowledge and culture.

There was a time in my life when I thought cultural nuances and our indigenous knowledge systems were hocus pocus, until 2010. The term indigenous knowledge generally refers to knowledge systems embedded in the cultural traditions of regional, indigenous or local communities, and in many instances this traditional knowledge is passed from one generation to the next through oral tradition.

A series of unfortunate events unfolded in 2010, not only in my life but in the lives of my siblings as well. I lost my job, Zihle, my youngest sister, was involved in a car accident and my brother suffered a stroke. At the time I thought nothing of it until early 2012. At the suggestion of Zinhle, I consulted a seer. This was after a series of things happened in my life that did not make logical sense.

I consulted one that was based in Midrand. I had never done this before, being raised by a Jehovah's Witness. I decided to take a leap of faith and go ahead with my consultation. When she threw her bones, with all three sisters there, the reading pertaining to Mom was the same each time. There was something out of kilter that we needed to correct.

For starters, when Mom died, we did not slaughter; we opted to buy a carcass from the butcher. We reasoned that meat was meat. We were told it was important to slaughter an animal, especially given the way my mother died. The seer told us that wherever she lay, her soul was not at peace and that we needed to do a ritual. The seer's suggestion resonated with me and my energy. She spoke in a language I understood. My siblings and I decided that since 2012 would mark 10 years of Mom's death, the ritual would be done that year as a form of thanksgiving. This time around, we did slaughter and the seer came and cleansed our home in Claremont.

She explained that ancestral clearing or cleansing comprises the learning and healing from inherited emotional issues, unhealthy patterns or unresolved trauma from our ancestral lineage. When something is out of kilter in the spiritual realm, performing a cleansing ceremony releases us from energetic patterns that are tied to our ancestors, patterns which can have a disruptive influence in our present life experience.

These healing sessions are important because we are impacted by emotional and energetic patterns, contracts or belief systems that were formed by prior generations in our families. Some of these unhealthy patterns can create obstacles in our lives, blocking our pathways to living up to our authentic aspirations, experiencing vitality and peace.

Ancestral clearing is therefore based upon the belief that what happened in a family's past is actually present and alive today within our cellular body and energy field. Consequently, any unresolved conflict from our ancestors, including unhealed emotional wounds, traumatic events, damaging thought patterns or belief systems and other limitations may still exist within our energy grid. This grid, due to our DNA, connects us to the larger energy pattern of our ancestors because energy is never lost. It connects us and it simply changes form.

Emotional issues that were not dealt with by our ancestors can hang in our energy field, creating imbalances and blocks. Ancestral clearing/cleansing can transform energetic patterns that are not good and are preventing us from carrying out our life's purpose.

The more the seer explained, the more it made sense to me. At this time, I'd been a yogi for six years and understood how energies worked. The ancestral clearing method is exactly how Reiki works – by aligning energies.

A few months later, I went to check in again with the seer if things were now spiritually okay with Mom. She threw the bones and I saw the bones that symbolised my mother were now much closer to the rest of the bones. What had also come out in my reading, versus that of my sister Nandi's, was that her guardian angel was Mom, whereas mine was Dad.

Little did I know that this reading was so spot on, when in 2013 all hell broke loose with the remains of my father. More about that later.

As such, I regard all forms of education important. Formal education broadened my horizon in terms of how I interact with my environment, scholastically speaking, while informal education taught me to have a broader view of things, for example how energetically connected we are as people. Toxic people, for instance, are energy vortexes. This is something I feel that has not been taught to me at school or anywhere else. It is something I gained by interacting with people.

Spiritual education that was imbibed by me taught me sound values in terms of morality and ethics, while indigenous education taught me to connect with my ancestors.

This has worked for me and made me the person I am today, the sum total of all forms of education I have received.

As I was gathering material for my memoir, I came across information regarding indigenous knowledge or education, as it were, and its role in my family.

Ntombizodwa, a daughter of Rhanuga, a cousin to Dalindyebo, talks about the education that Granddad received at Mqhekezweni. She tells Aunt Fatima:

I have told you about Nelson's education and his college. But there was another education that we received at Mqhekezweni and I believe it was important to him as it was to all of us. That was the education we received by simply sitting silently when our elders talked. We never made the slightest noise and our elders took no notice of us and it was as if they did not know we were there.

> *The chiefs and headmen from all the districts came to Mqhekezweni and when their business was done, they would sit in the dining hall and talk. As children we listened, and we heard a history that was not written in our schoolbooks. They spoke of Thembu Kings who had glorified the nation and Thembu Kings who had compromised and sold out to the British and reduced the people to beggars.*

To this day, this history, this education, is lost, as it is not documented. This is where Granddad cut his political teeth, in tribal council and the talks after tribal council.

Of all the people Granddad turned to for his informal education, it would be to Chief Zwelibhangile Joyi, who knew the history of the Thembus best of all.

Hence, I maintain all forms of education are equally important.

The lessons are not yet complete, as I am still learning.

Over the years, through a lot of soul searching, I have come to terms with the fact that dealing with death is a process that is continuously evolving. I have learnt not to second guess my feelings or hide my grief from the world. This is my personal journey and I have given myself the freedom to feel, think and say all that is needed in order to heal.

I am Ndileka and I am finding peace past the pain.

Chapter 10

Dealing with death

IN THE LAST 17 YEARS I have dealt with more death than I ever had before then.

The first devastating death in the last decade was that of Mom in April 2002. Since I had relocated to Johannesburg in 2000, I did not see her very often. In June 2011, she asked to see my children during their September vacation, and I had them spend time with her.

In December of the same year, 2011, I saw Mom at my cousin's wedding in QwaQwa. She was in high spirits and seemed very happy. The following year, early March 2012, at the funeral of Rundu's brother Samuel in Engcobo, she was depressed and had lost a lot of weight.

Two weeks prior to her passing, Nandi had called me to talk about her depression, as it seemed she'd got more depressed. We both agreed that after attending Josina Machel's traditional wedding, we would take her to seek professional help. In the meantime, I was to look for a psychologist for her, since this was my forte.

I am Ndileka

On 16 April 2002, I was about to leave work to go home when I received a call from Nandi telling me Mom was missing. At the time, Mom was working with Mam Khosi, tending to patients with AIDS who were bedridden and could not take care of themselves. They would meet every day around 10 am, get food parcels, go and drop the parcels off and often ended up giving these patients a bath. Mam Khosi had been calling Mom since 10 am, as it was out of character for her to be late. If Mom was running late, she would call and alert anyone she was to meet. This is what Nandi meant when she told me she was missing.

I drove home and told her to let me know when she had any news. I got home just before 5 pm. Another call from Nandi came with grimmer news. She had received a call from the police to tell her a body had been found floating in the Durban harbour, not far from where Mom's car had been seen. She asked me not to tell anyone until she had identified the body.

My heart sank and I started crying. My gut told me it was her mortal remains. Sensing my distress, Nandi repeated her instruction. She was looking for someone to accompany her to identify the body. I was more than 500 km away and could not give her the moral support. On the other hand, Zinhle was going ballistic, as she felt something was horribly wrong.

An hour later, the longest hour of my life, Nandi's dreaded call came through. It was Mom. Her depression had driven her to jump off the pier and take her own life. I decided not to tell my children until I had told both Rundu and Aunt Maki. Frankly, I did not even know how to tell them. Since Rundu was staying with Aunt Maki not very far from my house in Randpark Ridge, I decided to drive to her house and tell both of them in person.

On my way I called Aunt Beryl with the news. She was

married to Mom's elder brother, Sion. All she said was, 'Oh, my God, Thoko finally succeeded.' At that moment I chose not to ask what that meant but I understood it to mean she had tried before. By the time I arrived at Aunt Maki's place I was a basket case. After breaking the news, I just let go of my sobbing. I was more worried that my siblings were all alone in Durban with no family to give them moral support, as we were all in Johannesburg. Mam Khosi really came through for my siblings that night and every day since then.

Nandi had the unenviable task of breaking the news to Zinhle. I'm told Nhlanhla, our brother, was having a meltdown. When the news was broken to Zee, she had to be sedated. I could feel their pain from miles away. How do you reconcile the fact that a parent you had seen alive the previous night had woken up that day and had taken their own life? I could not imagine what my siblings were going through that night. I could only join them the following day.

For me, as a nurse and her eldest child, it was worse. I blamed myself as I felt, as a nurse, I should have seen the signs and sought out medical assistance for her. Was I so wrapped up in my own drama that I was blind to the turmoil she was going through? Did I drag my feet in finding a psychologist for her as Nandi and I had agreed on?

All these questions were going through my head that night, and I had to break this terrible news to both Tembela and Pumla. That night we also informed Granddad, who was in Maputo at the time to attend Josina's traditional wedding. Granddad asked Nandi and me to wait a week for the burial, as he wanted to be present at her funeral. Mom died on a Wednesday; we could not bury her that weekend anyway.

The following day, Aunt Maki and I flew to Durban to start with the funeral preparations. Our first stop was the state mortuary to identify Mom then transfer her to a mortuary of our choice. Mom looked so peaceful in her eternal sleep.

The whole 10 days before the funeral were just a flurry of activity. Aunt Maki left two days later, once the bulk of the preparations were made, that is, choosing a casket, a caterer and venue. My uncles, Mom's two elder brothers, also came to be with us to give moral support.

African mourning periods can be exhausting, though. We had a checklist and every morning Nandi and I would wake up and sometimes Zinhle would join us as we went about tying up loose ends, while my uncles and Nhlanhla remained at home to receive people who had come to mourn with us. There was no time for me to 'sit on the mattress'. I was told I should have, as I was the eldest, but I did not have the luxury of doing that, as it also fell on my shoulders to make sure things went smoothly.

Mom was Catholic and every night a Catholic priest would come to our home to do the evening prayer and service. I knew nothing about the Catholic Church, and still don't. During one of the prayer services, I noticed that they were repeating the same prayer. When I managed to slip to the bathroom, I quickly went to the kitchen to drink water and while there I asked Nokwazi, Mom's housekeeper, why they were repeating the same prayer over and over again. She then told me it was the rosary prayer. She asked me if I saw the beads they were carrying. I said yes, then she told me they have the same prayer for every bead. Lord have mercy. I decided to stay in the kitchen until I could gauge that they were on the last five beads so as to not to offend the priest.

The rest of the days before the funeral were spent making the preparations. Five days before the funeral, I had to send for my children, as they were still in Johannesburg. The day before the funeral, the ritual of washing the deceased's mortal remains and dressing them up fell upon me as the eldest of her children. Aunt Maki came with me. As I write about this, I remember it well.

We decided not to bring her mortal remains home the night before the funeral, as per her wishes. The morning of her funeral, her eldest brother, Aunt Maki and I had to bring her one last time into her house before the burial. Granddad and Mom Graça, Mama Winnie and the rest of the family came in their numbers to bid Mom farewell, but first we had to attend to culture.

Uncle Shorty, Mom's elder brother, carried *Umsimbithi*. This is a special branch carried to fetch a person's spirit from the place where they died until they are committed to the ground. The person carrying *Umsimbithi* starts talking to the spirit from the location of death and is not allowed to talk to anyone until burial.

This was no different for us. Before going to the mortuary, we started at the harbour, where Mom's body was first sighted. Uncle Shorty spoke to the spirit the whole time. Parts of the funeral process are a blur to me, as it was still very surreal that I would never see Mom again. She was still young, at 57 years old she was just three years older than I am right now.

After the burial, we all went for lunch and Granddad stayed and insisted that he wanted to see us back home after the lunch. I thought that was very sweet of him. That afternoon, when we all went home, I felt as if the walls were closing in on me.

We had been cooped up in the house for almost two weeks and I needed some air. I needed to breathe. I needed to process things. It was as if Aunt Maki could feel this, because she took us out for dinner. Mom was buried on a Saturday and the following day her lawyer came to read us her last will and testament. Late that afternoon I left Durban with my children, as they had to go back to school. They had already lost a week.

At Aunt Maki's suggestion, I went to see a therapist in order to process things. I was still in a state of shock. In fact, she suggested that we all go for therapy. I attended two sessions and felt that I did not need it, until Rundu died and I went into a deep depression.

When Rundu died, although she had sort of prepared us, her death came as a shock because she was still strong, albeit 82 years old. Rundu's funeral preparations were much easier on me, as I was not in the lead role. She also had the belief all Jehovah's Witnesses have that she would be resurrected on Paradise Earth, so she did not fear death, she welcomed it. Because of her extreme religious beliefs, I was able to handle her actual death better.

When Rundu died, I lost my anchor and felt rudderless. I had my meltdown three months after her funeral. I was driving from work in the afternoon and going to the gym at Health and Racquet and just could not stop crying. I asked Aunt Maki for a good therapist and she suggested Claudia. Once I started seeing Claudia, I never looked back. My road to self-healing began.

Uncle Kgatho's death seven months later sent me towards the deep end again.

We had a family ritual we had established from the time I relocated to Johannesburg of having Sunday lunch at Aunt Maki's house. The Sunday preceding Uncle Kgatho's admission to Linksfield Clinic, he'd told us in passing that he was to have a routine check-up. 1 December 2004 he drove himself to the clinic and was not to return alive.

I remember my reaction the day Aunt Maki called to tell me that he had complications after undergoing a cholecystectomy (removal of the gall bladder). In all my years of working in ICU, I had never seen a patient survive this operation, and I told her this.

The day after we visited him, he slipped into a coma and remained in that state for two weeks. Around 20 December 2004, he woke from his coma and we were all hopeful. Then a few days later, his condition changed for the worse. It was a Sunday and I had gone to visit him before going over to Aunt Maki to get started with Sunday lunch. I was chopping vegetables when I received a call to come back to ICU, as his condition had worsened.

While driving back to the hospital, I kept asking myself what happened, as I'd left him sitting in a lazy boy chair, ready for a walk. His breath was laboured but he seemed okay. Upon arrival at the hospital, I was told his oxygen saturation had dropped dramatically, falling below 60%, and they had to ventilate him again.

We had no option but to inform Granddad, who came rushing to the hospital. Granddad looked so vulnerable and frail. I'd never seen him this way before. He looked utterly helpless, as he pleaded with the doctors to do anything they could to save Uncle Kgatho. It was touch and go as we all held a vigil at the hospital with Granddad in the waiting room. The doctors managed to stabilise him after midnight. We all breathed a sigh of relief, although he was still unconscious.

My dear uncle never regained consciousness and died on 6 January 2005. That morning, I was getting ready to go to the gym when I received a call from Aunt Maki telling me that she thought her beloved brother had just died because the hospital asked us to come to the ward and she could pick up a tension in the nurse's voice.

We called Granddad. When I arrived at the hospital, the nurses were still laying him out, a procedure I knew so well

I am Ndileka

– preparing and straightening the body before rigor mortis sets in. None of us were prepared to give Granddad the news once he'd arrived. He kept asking if the doctors were still stabilising him. When Dr Su came in to tell him that after he crashed, they had tried to resuscitate him and failed and that he had joined our ancestors around 7 am, Granddad sat still. This would be the second son he was losing, and the pain was too much. The second loss was too much to bear.

I believe something in him died that day. He suddenly looked older and even frailer. By the time we were all allowed to go in and see Uncle Kgatho's body, there was a huge media presence outside the hospital.

That is the tragedy of our family, the tragedy of all families of struggle stalwarts, the fact that before you can process what has happened, the media swamps you.

Granddad insisted that Uncle Kgatho be buried in Qunu. By now my father and the first Maki who had died in infancy had been exhumed from Avalon Cemetery in Johannesburg to be buried in the Eastern Cape.

Later that day, we met as a family, as there was going to be a press conference at our home in Houghton. Granddad told us he was going to reveal that Uncle Kgatho had died of AIDS. About to turn 40 in February that year, for the first time I found my voice to speak back to him. I told Granddad that this was untrue, that he had died due to complications from a laparotomy, in my view. At no point during his entire illness and his hospitalisation was his viral load high enough nor his lymphocytes and CD4 count low enough to have full-blown AIDS. Granddad argued that it was important to declare this despite my medical misgivings, to further destigmatise HIV and AIDS. This happened during the President Mbeki administration.

This really angered me, as I felt that Granddad always

chose the country over his family. I felt that in this instance he should have been my uncle's father rather than the former president. The press conference happened as scheduled, and then came the preparations for the funeral in Qunu.

By the time the day of his funeral came, I was emotionally and physically drained. There was a lot of family drama that, in retrospect, I could have handled differently. I guess tragedy and death have a way of bringing certain things that have been bubbling under the surface to the fore. I will talk about these issues later when I talk about my years in therapy. I remember that after the lunch following his burial, all I wanted to do was to zone out and not feel the pain of his loss. In a way, I think I literally did zone out.

The Sunday after his funeral we all flew back to Johannesburg. Barely two days after we had buried Uncle Kgatho, I was involved in a serious car accident. It was a Monday, 17 January 2005. I had just picked up Pumla from her Irish dancing lessons and she was buckled up in the passenger seat next to me. When we reached the intersection of Jim Fouché and Beyers Naudé drive, there was a taxi in the extreme left lane on the opposite side of the road turning into Jim Fouché, and since there was no other car on Beyers Naudé, I had the right of way and proceeded to turn right into Jim Fouché.

The next thing I heard was a big bang on the passenger side and the impact bashed the door in so much that Pumla was almost on the driver's side of the car. By the grace of God, although the passenger door window was shattered, she had not even one scratch. She was screaming her lungs out for me to get her out of the car. I don't know where I mustered the courage to be calm. I got her out of the car. My instincts are usually sharp and ordinarily I would have checked again to see if there was no vehicle coming my way, although the taxi had signalled that it was turning. It was all part of the space I was in after Uncle Kgatho's burial – a bit out of it all.

I was also exhausted, as I am always hands-on when there is a ceremony or funeral in my family. You know how in all families you have the work horses and the commanders who don't do jack but talk the loudest and take credit after all the work has been done? Yep, we have these in my family too. I am the work horse in my family, and it is a position I do not mind, as it gives me an opportunity to do things the way I see fit, and, yes, I am a bit of a control freak.

There was a gentleman who was so kind at the accident scene and drove us home after the car was moved out of the way. Later that night, after I'd shared the news of my accident with my family, the enormity of the accident, the after-effects of Uncle Kgatho's funeral and the drama hit me, and they hit me hard. I was literally shaking. It was the day I started to have real respect for German-engineered cars. I was driving a Jetta back then and I learnt it is fitted with side impact bars that helped save Pumla's life.

The repairs on my car cost a whopping R80k but, fortunately, it was insured with a waiver for any excesses. It took panel beaters a whole month to fix it.

Things were entirely different when Granddad died. This time I wished he was not a former statesman and the global icon he was. In life he was hardly ever mine and in death he wasn't mine either.

Granddad's death was expected and, although in the end I was praying for his release, as I could not bear to watch him suffer any more, it was also peculiar. It was peculiar in the sense that eight years prior to his death, we started preparing for his funeral. This is taboo in the African culture but was necessary, as we knew he was not a fan of chaos and to avoid it we had to start early. He was involved to the extent of pointing out exactly where he wanted to be buried.

What millions of people saw televised during the 10 days of the mourning period declared by government was a result of almost nine years of work. A funeral like that took a lot of blood, sweat and tears. There was a lot of resistance, even within the family, but Aunt Maki and I pushed because we knew when the inevitable happened it would fall on our shoulders to pull it off. We started off as a big team with representatives from Granddad's five children in the Funeral Planning Committee (FPC), or Project Infinity, formed with the government, but most members fell off. Perhaps that was due to how heavy the subject of his passing was, not that it wasn't heavy for my aunt and me. We just chose to carry this burden on behalf of the family.

From the time Granddad took his last breath, I knew I did not have the luxury to wallow in sorrow. I had to be strong for my children, and Project Infinity (the FPC) had just been activated. Aunt Maki and I were the cogs in that plan from the family side. I was on autopilot from start to finish. Those in the FPC had always known that Johannesburg would be a breeze compared to Qunu in terms of coordination. There was no events management company hired for Qunu. The FPC was it.

Because we had to import all the infrastructure to Qunu, mourners were restricted to 5 000 people. This was due to safety regulations. We were going to have heads of state from various countries there and we were told if, for any reason, there was a disaster and these heads of state needed to be evacuated, we needed to limit the number of mourners. There was so much infrastructure in our homestead during those days of mourning, it looked like a mini town.

I was primarily in charge of accrediting close to 2 500

family mourners on the guest list, which was a nightmare at the best of times. I had created different Excel spreadsheets for different categories of close family friends. This list was drawn from people who had been with the family through all our ups and downs. It was also drawn from Granddad's close friends and comrades, people we had seen at various birthdays and had been around him most of his life.

Managing the spreadsheet became very challenging. For instance, there were different accreditation centres and I had sent the list to the main person I was dealing with at the State Security Agency who then disseminated it to the centres. I was permanently stationed at the Houghton accreditation centre. All the centres were under strict instructions that should a person's name not appear on any of the lists, they could not be accredited unless that was cleared with either Aunt Maki or me, family mourners, that is. Sometimes I would be in the middle of my duties and would receive a phone call that so and so is not on the list, and often I would know off the top of my head if that person was on the list or not. This is because I had started the list from scratch and had had eight years to familiarise myself with it. It also helped that I have a photographic memory. At times, though, I would have to physically go over my spreadsheet to find the names.

Family drama can be compounded during bereavement and our family is no different. Fortunately for me, the family drama I was confronted with came from issues of family guests being put on the list. I had asked all family members to give me their lists; some did, and some did not. I warned them that I would not accommodate them if they came at the last minute. Adding names at the last minute would be an administrative nightmare. When crunch time came, lo and behold there were family members who came scampering for their guests to be added. For the most part I did, but at times I refused point blank.

One afternoon, just before the daily prayer service in Houghton, a family member sent their guests to get photo accreditation. It had been a long day and I was quite stressed. This person was really causing a fracas, wanting to jump the queue, and I was having none of it. After a while, I asked them their name and they told me. I knew this person was not on the list, as I was familiar with the list for close and extended family members and I told them so. They asked me how I knew their name was not on the list. I looked at them with a deadpan expression on my face and said, 'Because I created the list from scratch, the person that sent you did not.'

There were also family members of some stalwarts who did not want to abide by the rules. One afternoon – this was the day before the official memorial service at FNB stadium – a stalwart's family member came in, jumping the line. People had been waiting patiently for their turn and things were running smoothly. When they saw that we were not having any of that jumping-the-line scenario, they called me outside to have a word. I got up, irritated, but went to hear them out. They told me it was unfair for them to stand in the line, as they regarded Granddad as their uncle and they were in mourning. Mustering my most calm voice I retorted, 'I have just lost not only a grandfather but a person I regarded as my father and I am here, doing accreditation. Do you think it is fair for me to be doing this?' Needless to say, they left. If they wanted to be accredited, they had to wait in the line like everyone else.

The following day, which was the day of the memorial service, the same person sent their driver to come and get their photo accreditation tag. Poor driver, he had to face me again, as he had watched his boss throwing a tantrum the previous evening. I looked him straight in the eye and reminded him of what had happened, then proceeded to ask, 'Having witnessed what happened last evening, do you think his accreditation card is ready?' to which he told me that he did not think so, as his boss had left without even taking the picture needed for the accreditation.

The day after the memorial service, the first day of Granddad lying in state was to commence. Straight after the viewing, I left with the team that was to precede the rest of the family members. Due to heavy rains we had to land in East London and be driven in a convoy to Qunu for the burial.

For two days it rained so heavily that some of the trucks carrying infrastructure got stuck in the mud. We were even worried that the dome would not be ready on time. Finally, the heavens cleared the day before the rest of the family members and the remains of our patriarch joined us in Qunu.

Every fibre of my mind, body and soul was exhausted, drained, but I had to push on.

The day of the burial dawned with clear blue skies. Around 6 am, I walked into my grandfather's room to bid him one last goodbye before a short family prayer service was to start. I still had not processed his death. Sure, his body was lying lifeless in a casket, but it was still surreal to me.

After the burial, I only went to the marquee where lunch was being served to greet my guests. I did not want to eat. All I wanted was to curl up in my bed and sleep for a week. The following day we all partook in a ritual that was to start our official mourning period, which was to be six months for us as his progeny and a year for his spouse.

I could not wait to be home and alone in my bedroom and let the sorrow wash over me. That evening back in my house I just collapsed into bed. For the next few days I received visits and calls from friends. A few of my German friends who had attended the funeral came to see me. But it was later that evening when a former boss and dear friend of mine called me that I let go. I could not even talk; I was sobbing uncontrollably. All he said to me was that I was to choose a destination anywhere in the world and go there for 10 days. He would pay for flights and everything. I chose Mauritius and jetted off on 27 December on an all-expenses-paid holiday, courtesy of Moss Ngwenya. Moss saved me from a deep depression.

I went there alone to process things and it was the best thing that happened to me because I came back rejuvenated. All I did on the island at a beautiful spa resort built along a Mauritian lagoon was read, swim, go for long walks, go for spa treatments, cry and watch movies. I cried until I had no tears left to cry, and I could do so freely, away from my children. At the end of the 10 days I was ready to resume and claim my life.

For three years Granddad had consumed me. My life revolved around him, literally. I was even scared to travel too far, out of fear that, should something happen, I would not be there to give him the energetic support he needed. I gave him support because my father could not. When he took his last breath, I wanted to be there, the same way I was when Rundu took her last breath. I consider myself fortunate enough to have been there for both my grandparents to the end, to their very last breaths.

The deaths of both my mother and Rundu, although difficult to handle, were not as bad as Uncle Kgatho and Granddad's deaths. I guess it was because their passing received public attention.

With Uncle Kgatho, a few minutes after he died, there

were journalists camping outside Linksfield Clinic. I have no idea how they found out and, as the days went by during the mourning period, there was more media attention. This was a challenge for me, especially because it was difficult to mourn under the constant barrage of cameras going in and out of our Houghton home. It was also difficult for me because I was forever in the thick of funeral logistics preparations.

The funeral proceedings were surreal and I was so occupied with what I needed to do after the burial, that, with Uncle Kgatho, I did not witness the pouring of the soil into the grave, as I had to leave with my sister and cousin to man the lunch marquee. I feel this is the most important part of closure, watching the entire gravesite ceremony.

With Granddad's death, from the time he died up until his funeral, we were all constantly surrounded by cameras. I can't explain how difficult it is to mourn with a lens trained on you half the time, notwithstanding the constant phone calls. It does not give you a chance to process things. You feel as if you are on stage all the time.

Granddad has been particularly difficult to mourn. I remember, when I came back from Mauritius, I saw a massive picture of him smiling from ear to ear at OR Tambo Airport. The sight hit me hard. For 10 days I had not seen his picture. For 10 days I had tried to process things, but seeing him like that took me aback. Most families are not confronted with seeing their loved ones in the media. Hearing his voice is like hearing from the dead, it is sometimes eerie and surreal. It is a pain I have learnt to live with.

When it comes to the mourning period, our family is no different from most South African families. We observe the mourning period the same way, except when Rundu died. Since she was a Jehovah's Witness, we did not observe any official mourning period. Come to think of it, even with

Mom, Ouma and Uncle Kgatho, I don't remember observing any official mourning period, but with Granddad we did.

The day after Granddad's funeral, after going to a nearby stream to wash one of his garments, we all assembled in one of the rondavels in our homestead to partake in the commencement of the official mourning period. We were all given buttons to wear and were also advised on how to conduct ourselves during this time. This conduct included abstinence from alcohol, parties, profanity and getting home too late. As the children of the family, we were to mourn for six months while Mom Graça and Mama Winnie were to mourn for a year.

It is actually now as I pen this book that I value the wisdom of our culture and traditions as pertaining to death and mourning. The abstinence of all the activities I have mentioned allows you to process death without distraction.

Thank God, in our family, women are not required to shave their hair. This reminds me of when my stepfather, Daddy Phineas, died. The Zulu culture and the family Mom had married into necessitated that she cut her hair off after Daddy Phineas died. Straight after the burial, which was in KwaNongoma, Mom was required to sit in the main bedroom of the house they had built there. The day of Daddy Phineas's funeral was extremely hot but, as tradition dictates, she was covered in a blanket, sweating buckets.

After the burial, she sat on a straw mat and they prepared to cut her hair. Mom had beautiful long thick hair. I left the room where this was meant to take place and went to mingle and change into comfortable, travel-friendly clothing. Straight after this hair-cutting process, we were all to drive back to Durban. Suddenly, my sister and I were summoned to the room and told Mom was not feeling well. When we walked into the room, Mom was collapsing and fainting.

One of my aunts told me we had to leave immediately and see to it that she saw a doctor. Of course, I was deeply concerned, and we quickly bundled her into the car and left. After some time on the road, Mom came to and started laughing. When we asked her if she was fine and what had happened, she explained to us that there was no way she was going to allow anyone to cut her hair. She would wear anything her in-laws required, for however long they wanted, but she drew the line on cutting her hair. We were in stitches. This is one of the things I miss most about her, her sense of humour. She went as far as feigning fainting to avoid cutting her hair. We would laugh about this incident even years after her own funeral.

Chapter 11

Relationships

MOST OF THE MISTAKES I HAVE made in life are in my relationships with people, starting with my relationship with my mother. I have learnt a lot about life in general and myself in particular from relationships.

I guess I never really forged a strong relationship with my mother. I can safely say that I never got over her marrying my stepfather, especially having to learn about her marriage not from her but from him. In retrospect, I don't think this was because she was negligent, rather because she was from a different era when children were not really part of adult decisions.

By the time I was in my teens, although I knew she had birthed me, she was more like a loving aunt I visited once a year, and because of this we were not that close until almost two years after my son, Tembela, was born. We also became close after the burial of my stepfather. As much as I used to go to Durban in my late teens to visit her and Daddy Phineas, Mom was often in Cape Town.

I was more Rundu's child and was used to her parenting style. I resented Mom's style. I resented how she would call me while playing outside just to change the channel on TV. She would be sitting right there, and I never understood why she wouldn't do it herself.

It was only after her death, through therapy, that I would learn that every parent does the best they can for their children with the tools they are given. It is also through my own parenting, and I have made my fair share of mistakes, that I know that being a parent is not easy. After her death, I appreciated my mother more and learnt the depth of her love for me. She made the best choice for me by allowing Rundu to raise me. My regret is that she is not alive today for me to tell her that.

As much as I made mistakes with Mom, I also learnt a lot from her. Mom had a sense of humour parallel to none. She had the ability to laugh at herself and laugh the loudest at her own jokes. Mom had this hearty laugh that came from her belly. When telling a joke, she would laugh herself silly before she reached the punch line, which could be quite frustrating.

Mom had a philosophy that no one owes you favours, not your siblings, not your friends, not your family. She believed that life does not owe you anything, period. I remember how we would lament that Granddad did not live up to a promise and she would tell my sister and me that he did not owe us a thing, that even if he had promised to do something and had not done it, for whatever reason, he and only he reserved the right to do so. Mom believed that even if I had, say, asked to borrow money from a friend or family member and they had agreed to do so and perhaps had not done as they promised, it was their money to begin with. They reserve the right to either loan it or not loan it to me. This is a lesson that has served me well in both platonic and romantic relationships: to let people be.

I have a friend who will always bemoan that a certain person has not invited her or called her, and I always refer her to what Mom taught me.

From platonic relationships I finally came to understand what Rundu meant when she did not want me to spend most of my time idling with friends. I was once betrayed in the most hurtful way in a friendship so that afterwards I vowed that only my sisters would be my closest friends. I did have one friend who knew most of my secrets. We all have that one friend who knows you at your strongest and your weakest, the type of friend who you'll have over for coffee to talk nonsense, gossip and be naughty with. Unfortunately, my ride-or-die chick betrayed me in the worst possible way.

The betrayal I'm talking about is not the type where your friend takes your man, but the kind of betrayal you never see coming. The one where you trust another human being so much that you cannot believe they have been talking about you behind your back, accusing you of horrific acts, until you get proof of that betrayal from none other than their sister. That is how I was betrayed by a friend. From that day onwards, I vowed I would never have that kind of friendship again except with my sisters.

I love the relationship I have with my sisters. Our relationship is not one where we talk every day. We have a carefree relationship that is not clingy. We allow each other to be our own people and to have our own space. My sisters will never rock up at my place and yell 'surprise!'. If Nandi or Zee is coming to Johannesburg, they tell me ahead of time, and vice versa. We all love our freedom and space. We are lone wolves.

Perhaps that is the reason why we have a blast when we see each other, chatting and catching up on the news till the early hours of the morning. We also do that on the phone from time to time. Of the three of us, Nandi is more like our mother. Zee and I like goofing around, which takes me back to 2012 when we were doing the thanksgiving memorial and cleansing ritual for our mother.

Since we had not slaughtered when Mom died, we decided to slaughter, and we bought a Brahman. When this heifer was brought home for slaughtering in Durban, we wanted to offload it next door so we could slaughter it in our backyard. The way to our backyard is either through our front door or our neighbour. We then told our brother, who was being assisted by his friends, to offload it next door. The heifer went completely wild when we were trying to offload it, to the extent that the van that was carrying it almost toppled over.

Eventually we decided to offload it in our front yard, much to our misgivings, as our driveway is not only steep but paved and there would be no soil to cover the blood to avoid flies after slaughtering. As they were offloading the heifer, Zee and I were busy giggling and saying that the cow was exactly like Mom in terms of its stubbornness, much to Nandi's annoyance, as she did not find anything funny about this. The more annoyed she got, the more we laughed until she chastised us to stop acting foolish. Zee and I are more free spirited while she is more serious, and we love her for it.

Losing our parents has also brought us closer together.

Of all the relationships I have had, it is in the romantic ones that I have been hurt the most. I guess this is because romantic relationships either mirror you or reflect what is lacking or what you have not dealt with in your life.

Perhaps my past romantic relationships will explain why I have never been married or contemplated marriage until recently. There is one relationship that almost made me lose faith in men.

It was 1990 and I was madly in love with a man. This was before I had Pumla. I had met him in Durban in 1989. He worked as an accountant for an FMCG company that had its headquarters there. When we met, he was based in Durban but was transferred to Johannesburg later that year. I was elated when I got accepted into MEDUNSA, as this meant we could see each other regularly. From the get-go he knew I had a child and he told me he had two sons and was not seeing or in a relationship with their mother anymore.

When I started at MEDUNSA, we did see each other frequently. He had a house in Marimba Gardens, Vosloorus, and I would often spend my weekends there. I loved him wholeheartedly and I am not the jealous type. If a man does not give me any reason to doubt him, I do not; but I do not take being lied to kindly. We had an easy-going and loving relationship, but he could never keep time.

One weekend when I was visiting him, he had promised we would go out early that evening. Late afternoon one of his friends popped in and they went out together to buy some beers. I decided to get ready for our evening rendezvous while they were gone. I dressed up to the nines and waited for him. It was getting late and way past the time he had promised to come back or for us to go out and I kept calling him. They had left the house around 5 pm and it was now about 8:30 pm.

I was hopping mad by then and had stopped calling him. Around 10 pm, I decided to turn in for the night but not in the bedroom where we used to sleep. I locked the door to the bedroom where I was sleeping. An hour later I heard him coming. When he did not find me in our usual bedroom he came to where I was sleeping and kept knocking, but I ignored him. When I heard him telling his friend, '*Ketlo moshapa*' (I'm going to beat her up), I jumped out of bed,

I am Ndileka

unlocked the door, threw it open and told him cheekily, 'Ng'shape ge' (Bring it on). He just looked at me and started laughing and shaking his head. To this day, I do not know how I would have reacted if he had gone ahead, as back then I did not even know where the closest police station was.

I have to say, though, that I should have trusted my instincts that something was not entirely right when one weekend he took me to his hometown, Heilbron, in the Free State. He had always told me he had a house there where his mother lived with his children and that his mother knew about us, yet when we went to Heilbron we did not sleep at his house but at a friend's house. You know when you are head over heels in love with a man, sometimes logic and reason escape you, as they did me at the time. I do not even remember pressing him for reasons as to why we did not stay at his house.

The answer to my niggling thoughts that weekend came to me in the most shocking and hurtful way.

After completing my final exams for my first year at MEDUNSA, I decided to spend a week with him in Vosloorus before I returned home to Durban, as I would not be able to see him the whole of December. He would leave in the morning and come back just after 4 pm and we would cook together, or he would come home to a cooked meal. I had arrived at his house on a Friday and was due to leave on the following Sunday. Since I had already made up my mind that I was not going back to MEDUNSA, I had all my clothes in two very large suitcases in one of his spare bedrooms.

On the Thursday of that week, as I was sitting in one of the bedrooms watching soapies, I heard a car parking in the yard and thought it was too early for him to be coming back from work. It was around 3:30 pm. What was more surprising was the voices of two women and the sound of the lock turning in the kitchen door. He would normally lock the door and leave with his key, as sometimes I would be taking a nap when he returned, and I hated being woken up. He was a snorer and I'm a light sleeper, so this was my way of catching up on my sleep.

Now, since the person seemed to have their own key, I assumed it was one of his family members or something. I remained relaxed as the two women came into the house first and then the bedroom I was in. One of them asked what my name was. I told her mine and then she told me hers. At that point I remembered that that was the name of his 'baby mama'.

This woman told me that she'd heard I was shacking up with him and that they were getting married in two weeks. I looked at her calmly and told her that he had told me nothing of the sort, save that she was the mother of their children. She also proceeded to tell me that he had been reluctant to go ahead with the wedding and that she could see it was because of me. As calmly as I could, I asked her why she was getting married, if that was the case, especially since he had been cheating on her. The irony of it was that he was cheating on us both, but at least I was oblivious to the fact until that very moment. She told me it was what their parents wanted, which explained why he could not take me to his house in Heilbron when we had visited.

She then went on a rant about how lucky I was, as she should beat me up and burn all the clothes in my suitcases because he had been spending money on me instead of spending it on his boys. I told her she could go ahead but she must know that everything in those suitcases was bought and paid for by Ouma.

Part of me believed she was making up this story about him getting married to her. I had his house keys and could visit any time I wanted and, up until that moment, he had not given me any reason to believe that he was seeing another woman, let alone her.

Upon checking the time, I knew he would be home any moment. I asked if she could park their car next door so as not alert him. I knew he would just run away and not face his mess and I was having none of it. I wanted him to tell me this woman was fabricating all of this. I asked her and her friend to stay in the bedroom while I went to greet him. I wanted to see his face when he saw his baby mama.

When he arrived, I greeted him and proceeded to tell him I had a surprise for him. He was light skinned. I have never seen a person let alone a man blush that much. His face went crimson red. All I said to him was, 'Tell me what this woman is saying is not true. Please tell me you are not getting married in two weeks.' I did not need an answer since his reaction confirmed what I had been told.

The feeling I had was like I had been sucker punched; my breathing became shallow. He went to the bathroom and locked himself inside for a while. He eventually had to come out to sort out his mess. His fiancée asked if I had any relatives in Johannesburg and I lied and said no. I was not about to involve any of them in my mess. By now it was around 7:30 pm. His fiancée was determined that I was to leave their house that night. I was sobbing uncontrollably. I had to pack whatever I had unpacked from my suitcases and be driven to Jan Smuts Airport, as it was called back then. By the time we reached the airport, the last flight to Durban had left. He pleaded with his fiancée to let me stay the night at their home and leave on the next available flight in the morning. She was having none of that. He then called a friend of his to come and pick me up and drop me off the next morning, as he had bought and paid for my ticket back home.

This time, I was not having it. I was so enraged and my

last words to him were, 'I want you to forever remember that I did nothing to you except love you and you had to do this to me.' I turned and left to call my mother from a payphone inside the terminal building. I could not even talk but managed in between huge sobs and hiccups to ask her to pick me up from the airport in Durban the next day. That night I slept on the benches at the airport and part of me died as I vowed never to love like that again.

I arrived in Durban with swollen eyes from crying all night. When I got home, he was calling me incessantly. It's amazing how, when you're still in love with a man, you are bound to be vulnerable to them. He was begging for forgiveness and had almost managed to convince me to give him another chance. He was telling me that his wedding was only to appease his mother, as his father had died and that it would be marriage in name only.

I was on the verge of giving in when one of his closest friends, whom I knew very well, called me. He told me not to believe a word he was saying. He explained that my ex was weak when it came to decisions like that. He explained to me that, if he truly loved me, he would have been honest with me from the start. His friend saved me. After that, I stopped taking his calls.

Four or five years later I heard he had divorced the woman I'd met at his house but was remarried. I had no regrets towards not giving him another chance, as the trust in our relationship would never have been restored. The love my mother gave me during this period helped me pick up the pieces in my life and, shortly after that, I met and fell in love with Pumla's father.

My relationship with Pumla's father lasted almost five years and we broke up for reasons I do not want to get into, for her sake. Suffice to say, he was unfaithful and very emotionally abusive. To this day, I can pick up signs of an emotionally abusive man. They include being controlling, isolating you from your friends and knocking down your self-esteem. Fortunately, God gifted me with bucket loads of self-esteem that no one has been able to chip away at.

After my breakup with Pumla's dad and having an on-and-off relationship with him, I decided to not be in a relationship for a while. This was around the late '90s. During the seven years I was not in a relationship, I dedicated myself to being a mother to my children. As these things happen, I met and had another relationship, but that ended the day my uncle died. There is something about death that brings certain things in your life into sharp focus. Uncle Kgatho's death showed me that the relationship I had then was not working. I called the guy I was dating, asked to meet him and ended it that night.

I think the other reason I ended it was that I was in therapy and a lot of issues were coming up in my sessions, especially about my relationship with men. The year Uncle Kgatho died I was to turn 40. My decision was a combination of things: turning 40, therapy, starting yoga the previous year and going on a spiritual journey.

I can safely say my relationship with myself started. I believe when I embarked on this journey of self-discovery, it was then that I started to get in touch with the essence of who Ndileka was. Before then, I was the sum of the influences present in my life. My life revolved around what was expected of me by my family and by society in general.

The road to self-discovery or to solidifying the relationship with yourself is not an easy one. There were moments of doubt, but I had to trust the journey. Yoga helped me a hell of a lot, as I learnt to accept who I was – the good, the bad and the ugly. I began to accept my shortcomings and learnt to be okay with them. The first form of yoga I did was Bikram. It is done in a hot room heated to 40°C, sometimes with up to 70% humidity. Although the heat allows your muscles to warm up nicely to allow for maximum stretching, it also pushes your buttons, as your body is wet and slippery, rendering it difficult to hold certain postures at times, which can be frustrating. It is also done in a room full of mirrors to allow you to look at yourself and come face to face with your fears and flaws.

As I continued with my yoga classes and was able to master my postures, I slowly but surely began to find my voice. Each yoga class is different from the next. One day I can be strong in my class and the next day I will be falling out of my balancing postures. As I began to accept the variance in my yoga classes, I began to take my class experiences into my life and learn that days and life experiences also vary, and I learnt to be okay with that.

By the time I reached my mid-forties, I was deep in my self-discovery journey, and I was beginning to search for my purpose in life.

All in all, all forms of relationships have taught me a lot about myself.

From my relationship with Mom, I learnt not to be quick to judge and to let people be themselves.

From my siblings and sisters, I have learnt the true meaning of unconditional love.

From romantic love, I have learnt to take the good and the not so good but to always strike a balance. Aunt Maki once told me, 'In any relationship, if you find yourself compromising more of yourself, it is time to walk away.' I now practise this with every relationship I have.

Contrary to what I thought when my relationship ended in 1990, I did fall in love again in 2012, coming back from a trip in Nigeria. Sadly, this relationship ended in 2016. I have remained friends with this man.

I'm a sucker for romance and love and believe one day I will find the one I am meant to spend the rest of my life with.

Part Four

Chapter 12

Expectations and challenges of being a Mandela

TO A LOT OF PEOPLE, BEING a Mandela is all fun and games, globe-trotting and loads of money.

Nothing could be further from the truth.

Before I tackle the challenges that come with my name, let me first deal with the expectations attached to it, expectations I did not ask for, but are asked of me nonetheless.

Most of the time I am expected to have also gone into politics, as if politics is an inheritance of sorts. How do I begin to explain that by the time I got to know Granddad, I was already a teenager whose life was being shaped by Evelyn?

How do I begin to explain that by the time Granddad was released, I was 25 years old and my identity was already crystallised?

How do I even start to explain to the vast multitudes of people who see me or my Facebook posts and think that I can assist them, whether financially or in connecting them to other individuals, that I am also having my own financial struggles and many more struggles? It is expected that because of my last name, I must have a solution. I'm here to tell you that I don't. I will explain in this chapter how having the 'Mandela' name does not automatically grant you a meeting or grant you funds.

How do I tell a person that says to me, 'This is not in the spirit of Nelson Mandela', that I am not Nelson Mandela, without being considered rude or abrupt?

How do I tell people who ask to take a picture with me when I am having the most horrific day that I don't feel like doing so? The truth is that I smile and bury whatever my feelings are and have the picture taken. The danger in that is that I then take out my anger on the wrong people, because anger and frustration suppressed over a long time can be toxic. Thank God I have yoga to take out some of my pent-up frustrations, but not all of them.

Being a child from this family is not easy. Not only have I struggled to have my voice heard globally, I have also struggled to find my voice within the family. I was expected to conform to the standards laid by those who preceded me and for the longest time I battled and was deemed a rebel or a delinquent. It was only in my mid-40s that I began to let that voice be heard, to be authentic to myself. You can imagine how difficult it must be for those who come after me to have their voices heard, if I, as the first grandchild, have battled with it for so long.

I am asked, 'How does it feel to be the granddaughter of Nelson Mandela?' The answer to that is that it feels heavy most of the time. I have learnt to navigate that heaviness and carry it lightly. Honestly speaking, sometimes I do feel like responding truthfully, according to how I feel on that day.

The expectations people have of what it is like to be me

far exceed my reality. For instance, travelling to various countries, as many have seen me doing, has not come with money attached to it. I go to countries representing my family or the Thembekile Mandela Foundation to gain exposure and visibility for the work I am doing. None of that has generated an income and yet I have bills like everyone.

I often get invited to attend functions, but very seldom do I get paid for these appearances. People will pay celebrities a fee for coming to their functions, as they bring value to the function. While I bring the same value, in some instances more, if I charge for appearances, people think it's '*UnMandela-like*'. Why? Because I supposedly have this ocean of money that pays for my time, fuel and make-up to attend this function?

It's a well-known fact that Granddad's estate was modest and yet people still assume that I have an endless amount of money. Coupled with that, three years prior to Granddad passing, I spent all my time next to his bedside with no income, which was a conscious decision. With the assistance of a handful of people who understood what my role was, and through digging into my savings, I survived. Even for a Mandela, savings do get depleted, especially if there is no income. Again: expectation vs reality.

Appearing on TV or taking pictures does not mean income nor does it mean I am suddenly on speed dial with Oprah, Barack Obama, Richard Branson or any of the people I have been seen with.

Only Granddad had the ability to pick up the phone, speak to a businessman and, by the end of the conversation, raise a serious amount of money. This is the very paradox of my grandfather. The paradox that while he could do that for the country, he did not do that for me, set me up in business with the very same people he was talking to.

I did not expect him to. I am a typical example of my upbringing. I was brought up to not expect people to fall and fawn over me and, as Mom always said, Granddad did not owe me anything. He paid his dues for how he got treated; I must pay mine. That is why I feel the expectations piled on me by society are unrealistic.

Where do I get this magic wand to wave and, hey presto, things happen? The truth is that I do not. If I did, I would spend the rest of my days whiling away time and not living my life's purpose. I thank God for my upbringing, although I have often wondered if my life would have turned out differently had I been given everything on a platter. It sure would have been nice, but I doubt I would have become compassionate enough to think about human suffering.

Some people will think I am being angry or bitter. I am just being realistic. The hype of being a Mandela far exceeds reality. It is exhausting to be constantly bombarded with these unrealistic expectations. Believe me, they are a daily occurrence.

Taking a picture smiling next to the pool in my complex does not necessarily mean I am having the best day of my life. It means I have a choice to see the beauty that surrounds me and be happy that I am still breathing. I might be having the most awful day because I don't have money to meet my rent or buy food. It just means that I have chosen not to let that consume me and I have chosen to have faith that God will never forsake me. The era of social media has created a life of duplicity – pictures not matching your actual reality.

On the one side there is a person who is trying not to get bogged down and sucked in by their daily struggles and, on the other, their escapism or trying to live up to the very expectations I am talking about. Ultimately, though, you are the author of your own book; you write, delete, rewrite and delete what you want. I guess that is what life is all about.

A lot of the times I also hear *'hayi uziyekele'* – loosely translated, this means that I do not want to use my Mandela surname as leverage on political or business connections. This could not be further from the truth. As I explained earlier, Granddad could have done that when he was alive and for reasons best known to himself, he did not. I am strictly talking about me here, Ndileka Mandela. It also not due to lack of trying.

Back in 2015, a year after I started and registered the Thembekile Mandela Foundation, against my better judgement, I succumbed to the notion that I was not leveraging my last name enough and called a known person in the higher echelons of the ruling party to assist me with raising funds for one of the anchor programmes in the foundation. That person told me point blank they could not, as they were also battling with raising funds for their own foundation. Although I was disappointed, my mother's words kept ringing in my ears: 'No one owes you anything.'

Other expectations come from friends and acquaintances. I have had friends – I say had, as I have learnt to cut such people from my energy field – who befriended me because of what they thought or expected the friendship to bring. The reason I cut such people off is because they are dangerous, they don't come with altruistic intentions but rather want to only take. I call such takers 'vortexes', as they suck your energy.

My nature is such that I am rarely suspicious of people and their intentions. I believe people are inherently good and will have to prove otherwise for me to believe differently. I also grew up in a village town where you trusted everyone, and times were different then.

Here's the thing, everyone has an agenda for meeting

people, for doing business with them, even befriending them, even me, and your agendas just have to find common ground.

Granted, the Mandela name does come with perks. It allows me to be able to ask Tyler Perry, for instance, to take a picture with me without worrying that he will rebuff me. It also allows me to travel and address people who sometimes do not know what I stand for, because I am the progeny of this iconic man.

I must share this though: these travels can bring about a rollercoaster of emotions. Sometimes, they are a nice way of escaping my reality, as I might be going through a difficult patch. I get to wine and dine and meet governors and premiers of different cities all around the world. This is such an adrenalin rush because you get to visit places that some people only dream of, and I become the envy of most, but sooner or later I have to go back to the reality I have escaped. The way I deal with it is that, as much as my reality does not match my trip, it gives me an opportunity to dream and that is where everything starts. Everything I see around me, the chair I'm sitting on as I write this book, the computer, they all started as an idea or a dream to whoever made them a reality.

Life for me as a Mandela has been a balancing act, and at times that balance can be extremely challenging.

Along with the expectations placed on me comes the challenge of having just about everyone in the country feeling like they have a right to comment on my family and on my life.

Again, how do you tell people who may think they know you based on assumptions and expectations that they have no right to comment about any part of your life because they know nothing about your struggles? There is a general tendency for people to think that because they knew Granddad's political and public life, they therefore knew him. Granddad's public life was very different from his private life and so is mine. In fact, I do not think of myself as a public persona at all.

These comments can be extremely annoying, as very few people know what makes me tick. By and large, my 'public family' knows what I stand for.

This frustration came to a head when upon being asked by a journalist if former President Zuma should resign, I answered in the affirmative. Oh! This made such a rah-rah, some even going to the extent of asking what my grandfather would say if he were still alive. Not one family member asked me that because they know what makes me tick. Let me clarify. I made that comment as me, as Ndileka, not a Mandela.

A challenge that I am still battling with is that almost everything that happens in my family becomes a public debate. No more was this evident than when I was one of the family members who were at the forefront of repatriating the remains of my father, uncle and aunt from Mvezo. One of the days we were coming back from the Mthatha high court, there was a debate on the radio about whether Mandla was justified as the eldest male grandchild to do as he pleased. As I listened to the people calling in, for once, I wished people would just butt out of our family affairs and leave us be. To debate and have an opinion about an issue that you know nothing about is, in my view, ridiculous.

This issue of repatriation is something I have always felt I wanted to talk about, as a record for my children and my children's children to know what happened years after I'm gone. Partly so as not to repeat it and partly to give context, as some people may think we woke up one day and decided to be the talk of the country.

When Granddad was being taken to the hospital on 3 June 2013, the ambulance taking him broke down. When I learnt about it and subsequently read about it, something about it did not sit right with me, spiritually speaking.

Granddad was so critically ill the previous night that I doubted he'd make it to the next day, but he did make it. I had seen during my nursing days in ICU that sometimes a patient would only let go after they had seen a certain member of their family. I had certainly seen it with Rundu, who only took her last breath after seeing Mandla. There seemed to be something stopping Granddad, at least in my mind and some of the family members, so we decided to go to Qunu to speak to his mother. I mentioned earlier that we would joke about how much of a mommy's boy he was.

We met with the elders in the family to find out how this was done, and were told it is done at daybreak, before the sun comes out. We did as instructed by the elders and went to both my great-grandfather and great-grandmother's graves at our family burial site. Since our flight back to Johannesburg was only in the afternoon, we decided to speak to a local undertaker to assist us in fixing the tombstones on three other graves, that is Dad's, Uncle Kgatho's and Aunt Maki's (the eldest one who died at nine months after losing a battle to meningitis and after whom the living Aunt Maki is named). The slabs had different fonts and were uneven.

I recall that when the undertaker came, he made a comment about how the slabs seemed not to have been properly sealed. I had heard rumours that the graves were indeed empty but could not believe that anyone would do that, allow my sister and me and the rest of the family to visit empty graves. I can only put what happened next up to the hand of God, for if we did not do what we did, Granddad would be lying next to empty graves.

We asked the undertaker to dig one grave to see if there was a coffin and, if there was, he could put the soil back and fix the slabs. After a while he called us and told us that they had dug deeper than eight feet and that there was no way there was ever anything buried in those graves. We were all shell-shocked.

Two years prior to this, my family had discussed the necessity of not allowing Granddad to lie alone in his chosen final resting place in Qunu and had asked my cousin Mandla to repatriate Granddad's children from our family graveyard to the 'new' burial plot Granddad had chosen in Qunu.

To be perfectly honest, I was first numb, then angry. We all tried calling Mandla, but he did not pick up. We then flew back to Johannesburg. I tried to call him again when we arrived in Johannesburg and he picked up. I asked him where he had taken the remains of my father, where he had reburied him, and he told me in Qunu. I proceeded to tell him he was lying, as we had dug up one of the graves and found it empty. He then asked me why he was not told about it before we did it, and I just lost my temper. I choose not to repeat the text message I sent him afterwards, as it is one of those things I wish I could take back.

He was given an ultimatum, to repatriate the remains or we were going to take him to court. Before going to court we decided to try resolve the matter amicably by having a family meeting where he could perhaps first explain why he had done this and then return the remains. The media, without knowing why we were having a meeting, printed a story that we were going to discuss taking Granddad off life support.

After explaining to the elders why he did what he had done, he agreed that if the undertaker could follow him to Mvezo, he would show him where the remains were buried, and they would be repatriated to Qunu.

Simple enough, right? This was not to be.

When we left Johannesburg, Granddad was quite critical, so as soon as Mandla had apologised, we took a flight back to Jozi. We thought by the time we reached Jozi the remains would all be safely buried where they were supposed to be in the first place.

When we got back, we found out that when the undertaker arrived in Mvezo, Mandla was nowhere to be seen or found and could not be reached on his phone, so the undertaker left. By now I was livid. As a family we had to take a strong stance, as the situation could not prevail. Even then we let him know that if he did not do as he had promised, we were going to take him to court.

We then lodged the papers and went to court. During all this time I was still dealing with a parent who was critically ill. For three days, we had to be stationed in Mthatha until the case was presided on and the court judgement given. I will never forget that courtroom experience. Imagine myriad cameras trained on your face, many with long-range zoom lenses at close proximity, constantly clicking. I swear some of those cameras could zoom into me from Qunu. At some point, our lawyer had to ask the judge to ask the media to stop the constant clicking, as we could not even hear the court proceedings.

After being granted permission by the court to exhume the remains and rebury them in Qunu, we left immediately to go to Mvezo to them. Even when we arrived in Mvezo, the media could not allow us the courtesy of first finding out where the remains were and later exhuming them before they descended. It was like a scene out of a movie, with media crawling around with cameras and us chasing them away. Some were climbing over kraals, a cultural abomination.

We did not know where exactly the remains were buried,

as Mandla was nowhere to be found, again. I recall having this sick feeling that we would not find where they were, as we had been looking for a while and it was getting late and dark. I could not imagine going back to Qunu without finding out where the remains of my own father were.

My aunt would tell me later that it was upon receiving a call that she found out they were not buried in the yard but outside the walls of our ancestral home. There we found all three of them. It was easy to identify them. The first grave excavated was that of my uncle. I could still see his features, as he had also been embalmed as my father had been. Forty-four years after I had seen my father lying intact in his coffin, I came face to face with his bones. It is by sheer strength that I have put this horrific experience behind me.

I can still hear Aunt Maki saying, 'If something had happened to Mandla, I would never know where my own siblings were buried.'

It was the most painful thing for us, for me, and yet I heard people judging and making hypotheses and assumptions about our decisions without knowing the facts.

What boggles my mind to this day is how patriarchal our society is. Of all the people who were saying Mandla was justified, most were men stating that he was the oldest male grandchild. But I am 10 years older than him, and here I am talking about my father.

This gravesite story will give you a glimpse of what I am talking about when I mentioned that people make suppositions and talk about things they have no business talking about just because Granddad was a public figure and they feel they have a right to.

Where does his public persona begin and end? Where does mine begin and end?

I have learnt to make peace with this story and with the

many assumptions and expectations that people have of me.

I once saw a bumper sticker that said, 'What you think is none of my business.' In fact, I think Dr Wayne Dwyer says that in *A Course in Miracles*. I truly live by that bumper sticker, as I have learnt I just cannot please everyone.

Besides, I believe that the older I get, the more inclined I am to live my truth no matter how it looks to the next person.

Chapter 13

Being homeless

BEFORE I GO DEEPER INTO THIS chapter let me first explain what 'homeless' means in my context, because I know for most people it may mean roaming the streets.

My homelessness means I did not have a home to call mine. For just over three months, in 2012, I had what I'd like to call temporary addresses, plenty of them. Now let me start at the very beginning of how I got to be in this predicament.

When I moved from Durban to Johannesburg, I had to sell my property in Pinetown to enable me to buy one here in Johannesburg. I had lived in that property for 10 years and when my daughter started high school at St Mary's School, I had to relocate, as the commute between Randburg and Waverly was too far. I remember one morning it took me an hour to drop her off at school because of the heavy traffic.

I then began the process of putting my townhouse up for sale. Granddad had assisted me in buying this house with cash, so there was no bond on it. I started this process mid-year in 2009. It took long, as the person whom I had enlisted to help me sell was a friend and was not getting me the price I wanted. I ended up getting an estate agency to sell it, which earned me a bit of animosity with my friend.

I decided to do this on my own without asking Granddad's lawyer. It was important for me to do it on my own. I was soon initiated into the differences in price between Morningside and Randburg. I also learnt the importance of location when buying a property for the resale value. If the townhouse in Randburg was in the Sandton area, it would have fetched a much better price and would have saved me the biggest mistake I was to make as an adult in buying property.

I happened to mention to my then boss that I was doing this, and he offered to assist. He was a dear family friend and I suppose because we had dated years before I started working for him, he still had a soft spot for me. He also was very fond of Granddad and is a very generous man.

While my house was still up for sale and I did not have a buyer yet, I started house hunting and settled on a cluster in Morningside. I later had a buyer, but they still had to secure a bond for the sale to go through. In the meantime, I needed 10% of the purchase price to secure the cluster in Morningside. I spoke to Uncle Isaac who agreed to advance me the money.

My boss also threw in a substantial amount of money. I was only going to need a small bond, which I could afford, as I was earning a good income. My uncle asked a lawyer friend of his to assist me to register the bond. We got into the process of applying for the bond. I then signed the papers for the offer to purchase and the date to move into the house.

All this time I was banking on the money that would come from my boss, the purchase of my house and the deposit my uncle had advanced me to secure the bond, but when the money from my boss came, it had been taxed by 40%, as is law for donation tax, I was told. This was a huge setback, as the bank then wanted me to raise an extra 250k for the bond to be registered.

The date for moving in was drawing close and I could not renege from the sale of my house, as my buyers had since secured the bond and their agreed-upon move-in date was also drawing close.

This is where it all gets complicated. Since I still needed to raise the shortfall for my bond to be registered and I needed to vacate my house, I spoke to the owner of the cluster to allow me to move in. To sweeten the deal, I decided to also pay the amount donated by my boss as part of the deposit. This was the biggest mistake I made, as the contract for any sale, at least back then, stated that if for any reason the sale falls through, monies paid towards the deposit will be forfeited.

I was quite sure I would be able to raise the shortfall needed to register my bond. Now, over and above the money paid towards the deposit, I had to pay occupational rent until my bond was registered and the cluster was registered in my name at the deed's office.

I moved into the house in Morningside with my children amidst all the uncertainty, but I was still sure I was going to sort it out. Neither my children nor my siblings knew any of this. We moved into the house in November 2009.

When the money from the sale of my house became available, it was being paid to my seller to cover the occupational rent. Meanwhile, I had hit a stumbling block with the bank towards mid-2010 and on top of that my contract with my work came to an end. In fact, it had ended about six months prior to that, but there was another project in the pipeline. When that project fell through, my employment ceased in September 2010.

I was getting more worried, as the money from the sale

of my house was being utilised for the occupational rent. I wasn't that worried though, because I seemed to remember that all the occupational rent money would go towards the sale of the house, as per verbal agreement with my seller. The nagging feeling at the back of my head to get things sorted out refused to go away and I knew I needed to do so as a matter of urgency.

It was then that I decided to ask for assistance from Granddad. His health was starting to fail him even back then. Since he could not personally assist me, he solicited the assistance of a known South African businessman, whom he called to our home in Houghton to speak to. The businessman agreed to assist and asked me to call him the next day. This was around early November 2010. I called him almost every day for three weeks to no avail. I finally gave up.

I had now been living in the property for more than a year and the funds from the sale of my house were almost depleted. Then came January 2011 with its own set of challenges when Granddad fell seriously ill.

Shortly after Granddad was discharged from Milpark Hospital, I received a letter of eviction from my seller. By now all the proceeds from the sale of the house in Randburg had been depleted but the money for the deposit, which was about R800k, was still in my seller's conveyancing lawyer's account.

Naively, I still thought I could recoup at least about R500k of it since I had paid more than the 10% deposit needed. When I received the letter, I lawyered up. The lawyer whose services I solicited assured me that this was a winnable case and that, at the very least, my seller should pay me back the amount I had paid over the 10% deposit needed.

He wrote to the seller's lawyer stating this and we got the response that all monies paid were to be forfeited. My lawyer wrote back stating that this only applied to the 10%, but it was not considered. He told me to stay put until they had paid me the surplus above the deposit, and I did.

Unbeknownst to me, they then applied formally for an eviction order that was delivered to me around June 2011. I had no job, Granddad was ill and, being a nurse, I knew it was only a matter of time before he passed.

Have you ever been in a space where you are overtaken by events and you seem paralysed to do anything about what is happening? This was such a time.

The court had given me one month to vacate the premises and I had to look for a place where my children and I could stay. I found one and it needed two months' deposit for the rent. Since I had no job and had been unemployed now for almost a year, I could not go to the bank or to Granddad.

My only option was a loan shark. I went to one I knew and borrowed enough money to pay for at least five months' rent, including the deposit, by giving up my car. My reason was that we could not sleep in a car. This car was also paid off with the assistance of my now former boss and Granddad, and it was still basically new, as I had owned it for only two years.

In August 2011, we moved into another three-bedroomed cluster in Morningside. I managed to pay my rent after the five months through facilitating meetings here and there. By now it was clear Granddad's health was not good at all and I had also decided that, although my financial situation was precarious, I would take a sabbatical to be by his bedside. I also got financial assistance from friends who understood my decision.

I can honestly put up to divine intervention the reason for my survival from August 2011 to August 2012.

In August 2012, I got evicted again for not meeting my rental payment. This was during Pumla's gap year and she did not suffer the consequences of this much, but Tembela did.

This was the period when I entered the phase of 'homelessness'. I put all my furniture in storage, and we packed what we could use for a few months in suitcases and moved to a two-bedroomed furnished apartment for a week, to allow me to regroup. I shared a bedroom with Pumla while Tembela had his own room. This was a far cry from each one of them having an en-suite bathroom, but it was still comfortable living. These were nicely furnished apartments in Sandton. We were technically homeless, but we were not on the streets.

We would sometimes stay for two weeks, but we moved from one furnished apartment to the next in the Sandton area, depending on the availability of such apartments. This had its inconveniences, as we had to literally live out of suitcases. My children adjusted to this life grudgingly.

In September 2012, when my sisters found out about my predicament, they tried to assist by telling my aunt. A meeting was held at my aunt's place and it did not end well. This 'intervention' caused a temporary rift in my relationship with my sisters. I felt it was not their call and I was annoyed to no end. As the eldest of them, I wanted to mop up my mess myself. I had got myself into this mess, and I was going to get myself out of it.

These were challenging times for us as siblings. Fortunately, we have been able to mend our relationship and our bond is much stronger.

After about three months of not having a stable base, I finally found a place to rent in Morningside, which is where I am currently staying. I am now well on my way to buying my own home. It has been a long journey, but I have realised that life is full of these ups and downs. I heard this in a film, *Jumping the Broom*, and it stuck with me: 'The music may stop, but that doesn't mean you have to stop dancing.' I have learnt to dance in the rain.

Chapter 14

Depression

I FIND THIS TOPIC TO BE ALIEN in the African community. If depression as an African person is alien, try depression as a black woman. This notion is much more alien. Depression amongst black South Africans is largely understudied due to myriad factors, some of which are cultural and often because of language barriers. Perhaps this may also be due to the fact that it is thought that black people have a higher tolerance level for stress.

A lot of black people may not even be aware that they are suffering from depression, but if you find yourself experiencing a persistently sad or anxious mood, feeling restless and irritable, sleeping too little or too much, feeling guilty, losing interest in activities you formerly enjoyed and having thoughts of suicide, you may be suffering from depression.

While growing up I never heard of anyone being depressed. Maybe this was because it was viewed as 'normal' within the community I grew up in. It was assumed that suffering was intricately connected with the black community. I can't even understand where this came from or what it's based on, only that as the black community we have a higher tolerance for suffering and, therefore, depression. Another factor is that when I was growing up, the extended family support was readily available.

If, for instance, a family member was suffering some hardship, they could be shielded from embarrassment by family members who were more affluent. Families were able to assist each other, as they relied on subsistence farming, which was robust with plenty to go around. This is what made us unique as Africans, as black people – the ability to shield one another from pain and suffering. However, this has been eroded by urbanisation and political uncertainty in recent times, which have led to increases in poverty, violence and disturbed marital and social relations among the African community.

In a study called the 'Epidemiology of Major Depressive Disorder in South Africa (1997–2015)' by Nglazi MD, Joubert JD, Stein DJ et al, it has been shown that there are certain factors that can predispose a person to developing depression, such as high amounts of environmental stress and a low socio-economic status. There may be other factors, but apparently these two count for an elevated prevalence of depression in the black community. The disadvantaged position of the majority of black South Africans as a result of discriminatory socio-economic policies is still a major problem with grave consequences, one of which is the escalated occurrence of mental illness.

It has also been found, and this I believe, that many think of depression as only 'the blues', or a sign of personal weakness, rather than an illness. This belief is more prevalent in our African communities and especially where women are concerned. Black women are viewed as nurturers, caretakers

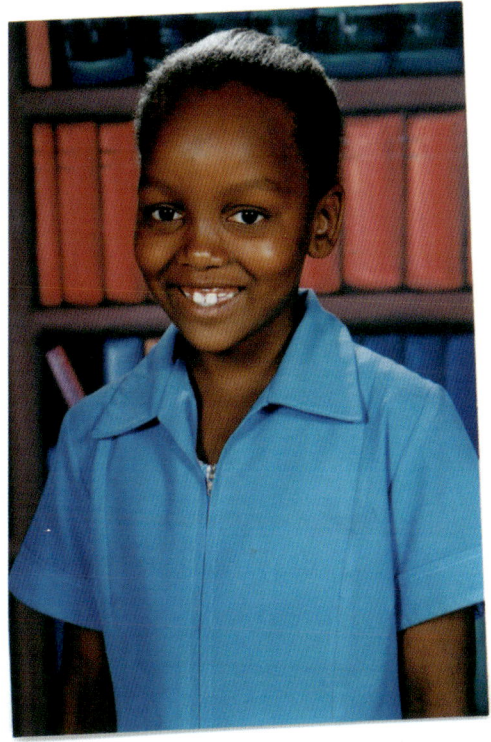

School portrait of Pumla at Rand Park Primary

Tembeka fresh from initiation school

Top left: Uncle Kgatho at Madiba's 87th birthday in Qunu

Top right: Ndileka and Thoko in 1998 at the reburial of Thembekile's remains in Qunu

Bottom: (Left–right) Zinhle, me and Nandi at my 40th birthday

(Left–right) Nandi, Mandla and me at Tembeka's initiation school

(Left–right) Zinhle, Nandi and me on Nandi's wedding day

(Left–right) Me, Tukwini and Nandi at a dinner event

Top: Grandad and me at the voting station; his last vote was in the 2011 elections

Bottom: Me embracing Granddad at his 88th birthday

Top: Me at the Ethical Leadership Summit at Tshwane University of Technology on 19 July 2019

Bottom: With South African ambassador, Shirish Soni, and his wife, Ruweida Soni. I was awarded a metric certificate for my social commitment to protect human rights by Alan Fabbri, mayor of the city of Ferrara, Italy.

Top: Total shutdown campaign in August 2018

Bottom: At the Houghton Muslim Academy on Mandela Day 2019

Left: Nandi, Pumla and me at the commemoration of the 50th anniversary of the death of my father in Touws River

Right: Me and Pumla at the University of Cape Town for Pumla's graduation, April 2019

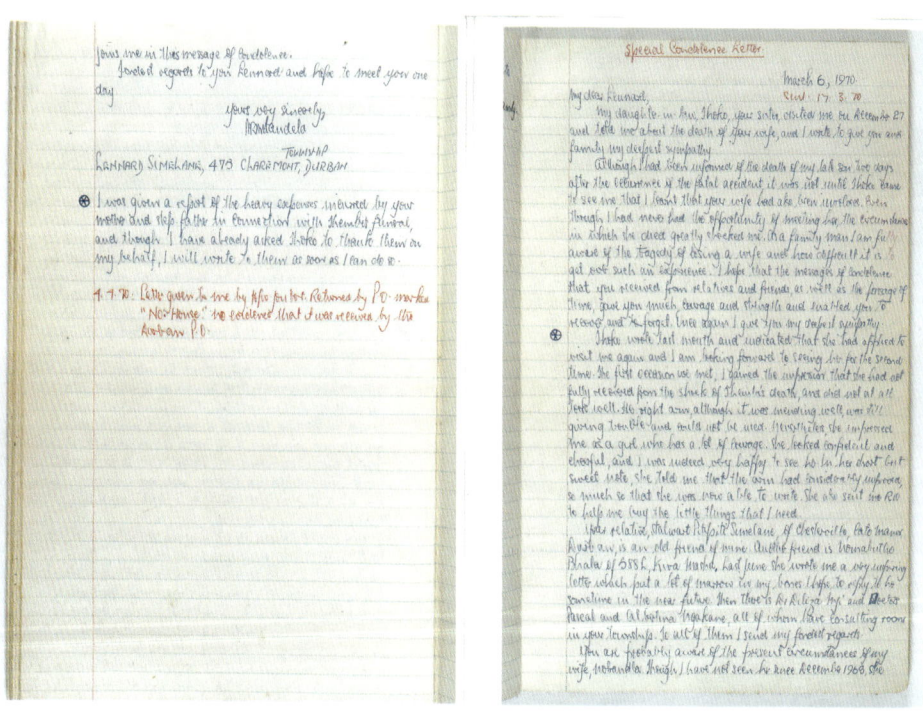

Letter from Madiba to Lennard (my uncle) after hearing Lennard's wife was also killed in the fatal accident along with Thembekile

and healers of other people and are supposed to be strong. When a black woman is depressed or suffering from a mental illness, the overwhelming supposition is that she is weak. This has serious implications, especially when one considers that depression is twice as high in women than men.

I believe there is a strong link between PTSD and major depression. If I have to use my mother's example, for instance, she was the sole survivor in the car accident that took not only the life of the love of her life, my dad, but her sister-in-law, Aunt Irene Simelane. I have never heard anyone tell me that after surviving this traumatic experience she went for therapy to deal with the loss. She never even talked about seeking help after the accident. I think her three suicide attempts before she succeeded the fourth time were linked to PTSD. I can't be sure of this exactly but my stint with psychology and psychiatry during nursing supports this hypothesis.

People who have experienced or witnessed catastrophes that were deemed to be outside the range of normal experience, like 'necklacing', political street violence, burning of property and gruesome accidents, have a higher chance of developing depression. This supports the scenario with Mom.

While I am not sure if I was clinically depressed or not, all I know is that one afternoon while driving back from work four months after Rundu was buried, I just could not stop crying. I had a sense of heaviness around me that I could not shake off. All I knew was that I needed help as this darkness I felt was threatening to swallow me alive. I remember calling my aunt and she referred me to Claudia, who was to be my therapist for almost three years.

This is where cultural nuances come into the picture. Prior to my seeking professional assistance, I would have brushed off the sense of darkness as 'the blues', as there were times when I had felt like that in the past but managed to 'bring' myself out of it, as most black women do. You feel low, give many reasons for it and figure out that you never heard your mother or grandmother talk about being overwhelmed or depressed, brush it aside and continue with your life. Only, this time, the darkness refused to go away and the one person I could talk to, Rundu, was no more.

The day I started my therapy sessions was on a Wednesday morning. I cannot remember what we talked about on that day, but as the therapy progressed a lot of the issues I was angry about and had kept bottled up came out.

One thing was clear, I had not resolved issues I had with my mother and I had serious daddy issues revolving around Granddad.

The issues around Mom centred on feeling abandoned by her. I felt that throughout my life she was never there for me when I needed her the most. I needed her to have told me when she remarried instead of hearing it from Nandi. I needed her to be there when I had my first menstrual period. I needed her to be there when I fell pregnant and had my first child. I buried all this disappointment until it festered into anger and drove a chasm between Mom and me for the longest time. Yes, Rundu gave all the love she could give me, and I never doubted it for one second, but I still wanted my mother to have been there for me.

During one of my sessions with Claudia, while I was spewing bile about Mom, she suddenly stopped mid-session and asked me something completely unrelated to what we were talking about. I was in the middle of a tirade about how Mom was not there for me when Uncle Kgatho was critically ill and I was struggling with his illness. She asked me who used to wear a necklace, and I proceeded to ask her what type of necklace, as I remembered Ouma wearing a pearl necklace. She then told me that it was a necklace that had a pendant and the wearer used to swing it back and forth. I told her it was Mom. She had an amethyst stone necklace which she used to swing like that, and I had taken it as mine when she died. Claudia then told me that the person wearing this necklace was sitting next to me.

I had goose bumps and my hair stood on end. She then explained that I may have thought that Mom was never there for me, but she was right next to me at that moment. I had never told Claudia about the necklace and back then I was a bit sceptical when it came to such things and, frankly, I never thought a therapist could have such vision. Slowly, I began to deal with my resentment towards Mom until it disappeared. Through my therapy sessions, I came to understand that as parents we use the tools available to us at the time. I began to understand that allowing me to be brought up by Rundu did not mean Mom didn't love me but that she felt I would benefit the most from being with Rundu, and she was correct.

What also came out during my sessions was how I blamed myself for Mom's suicide. I believed that, since I was a nurse, I should have seen the signs that she was depressed. Claudia explained that there is nothing one can do when a person decides to take their own life.

I also never realised I had a lot of daddy issues, and this was expressed a lot in my challenges with Granddad. Since Dad had died when I was very little, Granddad became a father figure. Claudia explained to me that Dad dying when I was four years old signified to me that men always leave. When I was growing up, men were starkly absent in my life. I was constantly surrounded by women, and strong women at that, or women who had a lot of male traits in them.

At the time of Uncle Kgatho's hospitalisation, my

relationship with Granddad was strained. As mentioned earlier, the illusion that I had about my relationship with Granddad was shattered when he was released from prison, as he became a grandfather to the entire world and not just mine. During one of my sessions, Claudia asked when I had last visited Granddad and I retorted, 'What's the point, we never talk about anything of substance anyway.'

She asked me what I meant, and I explained to her that our conversations were mainly centred on three questions:
- How are you?
- How are the children?
- How is work?

And up comes his newspaper that lets me know I am being dismissed. Claudia then asked me what stopped me from bringing my own book or magazine so when he did that I could read whatever I had brought with me. Up until then, I believed communication was only about talking but Claudia demonstrated to me that sometimes communication is about sharing energy and space with a person. Again, slowly, my relationship with Granddad began to improve to the point that I felt it was necessary to take a break from working when he got ill in 2011.

I can safely say that therapy assisted me with a lot of things, chief amongst them preventing me from going on medication. Thank God I got help. A lot of black women are not that lucky. They suffer in silence for very long periods, sometimes never getting help. I do not understand why we are thought of as being strong and able to withstand anything.

One of the things we have to withstand, for instance, is when husbands die, whether by accident or illness. A lot of the times in African cultures, the wife is suspected of having killed her husband through witchcraft. While dying is certain for all human beings, in the African culture, a wife must die first. I have never heard of a man being suspected of witchcraft when his wife dies. This compounds depression in the black community. Can you imagine that while you are dealing with losing your husband you have to contend with suspicions of being a witch? Often, the widow receives no sympathy from her in-laws or her female counterparts.

The thing about depression in the black community and amongst black women is that it is seen as a personal weakness. Many people never go for treatment, like my mother for instance, for fear of judgement and the stigmas of mental illness, especially if these stigmas are bound to cultural beliefs and religion.

Because depression is something that not only touched me personally but took my mother to an early grave, at the young age of 55, a year older than I am right now, I had to go a little deeper and read more about it, especially pertaining to the black community. I have learnt a lot.

I never heard Jehovah's Witnesses talk about or refer to mental illness or depression.

The stigmas are not only cultural but social as well. If you are depressed or suffer from mental illness you are told to pull yourself together. I know I did tell myself that many times before seeking medical assistance.

Although I believe in Western treatments for depression, I also argue that both spiritual healing power and ancestral belief cannot be disregarded, especially in the black community. To illustrate this point, I quote my cousin Dumani Mandela, in his book, *Rain on a Sunny Day: Living and Thriving with Bipolar*. In Chapter 2 of this book where he deals with 'The Black Experience' he says: 'As a young Black man, I knew that the cultural component of my illness had a major influence on how I wanted to be treated. There was a time when I wanted to see a sangoma rather than a psychiatrist because I was convinced that I was going through some spiritual crisis.'

He then explains that after his parents found him a black psychiatrist who understood some of the cultural paradigms, he started to get better, as this practitioner helped him with his illness as a black man and had a different tonality and a holistic method of treatment.

He goes on to explain the black experience:

The Black experience to me was not some ominous concept; it was at the centre of how I lived my life. It was how I spoke to my elders, how I treated others, what my expectations of my life were and also how I worshipped. My Blackness in itself is not my culture, but how my parents lived and how their parents lived, forms my consciousness as the black experience. I felt that my treating practitioner had to understand that in all of its forms and he did. It was easier for our parents to live the Black experience than it is for us now – and find value and meaning in it. The South African education system is still focused a lot on European culture and the Western lifestyle, culture and norms are fast erasing those of the African. To experience and appreciate the value of the African way of life, one would have to live in the rural areas or former homelands.

African culture had coping mechanisms for illnesses like bipolar that are now becoming fast forgotten; slaughtering for the ancestors, performing cleansing rituals or in some cases, people becoming sangomas. As those traditional coping mechanisms are being forgotten, many of us in South Africa are opting for Western treatments of mental illness. I am not saying

African treatment is better than Western treatment; I am arguing for the marriage of the two forms so that the Black experience can be treated in a holistic manner.

To me, part of the illness has to do with the fact that we are forgetting who we are and what makes our culture so rich and diverse as Black people. I think another part of the illness is a spiritual reminder of where we come from, how we are to live and how we are to pray. That is why I felt I had to get a Black doctor, so I could deal with the Black experience in entirety while accepting Western forms of medicine and treatment.

It is not popular in South Africa to be tribal, but I would argue that in order for young Black people to recover from bipolar, they have to be treated culturally as well as with Western science.

Since bipolar is a lifelong illness, why not accept that part of treatment is about culture which also stays with us for a lifetime. Science cannot separate a person from their culture and if it attempts to do so, it is at a patient's peril.

For me, Dumani's point brings to the fore our indigenous knowledge as black people and as a community. In treating depression and all forms of mental illness, I also argue, like him, for the marriage of cultural, spiritual and Western forms of treatment.

The bottom line is that depression and mental illness are real and, yes, they are real amongst the black community too. If you are going through any signs of depression such as persistent irritability, sadness or anxiety, feelings of hopelessness, guilt, helplessness, trouble sleeping and changes in appetite, as well as accompanying thoughts of suicide, please get some help. I did and so have countless other people who are managing their depression. Many people find strength and support through their religious and spiritual communities or through a support group.

Depression took my mother to an early grave and it had me contemplating suicide at one point in my life. I felt it was important for me to deal with this topic as it not only affected me directly but has affected my family as well.

Chapter 15

Being a woman in South Africa today

IDEALLY, BEING A WOMAN in South Africa should be great. After all, we live in a country whose Constitution lays down in Article 1 the fundamental values on which the Republic is founded and includes among them non-sexism. The equality clause of the Constitution includes a proviso that is aimed at ensuring substantive rather than merely formal equality: that equality includes the full and equal enjoyment of all rights and freedoms. Ours is a country that advocates for balanced gender representations in workplaces in both the public and private sectors, inspiring many other nations to follow suit. South Africa is a country that encourages and endeavours to support women participation in its economic activities and development.

But with this rich history and these ambitious efforts, we are still facing struggles as women. Many of our struggles are obvious to all of us; for example, we do not have to spell out the statistics of rape, abuse and murder, or that there are not enough women in decision-making positions in organisations.

There are certainly other struggles that I believe are less conspicuous but are there nonetheless. It is for that reason that Women's Day, or Women's Month, as it has become, calls for debates and conversations. It represents so many different things to so many different people, and aptly so, because we are all different as women and constantly have to negotiate fitting a certain mould.

Some believe that women in South Africa should aspire to have careers, husbands and children, and be able to accord equal attention to all of them – basically, aspire to super womanhood.

But looking around us, chatting to friends or watching television, we realise that the notion of a superwoman is hard to reach, if it exists at all.

Then there are those who believe that to be a woman in South Africa 25 years into the democratic dispensation, you need to set your sights on the highest peak of your career, climb that professional ladder and stay grounded in the knowledge that you are phenomenal all on your own and do not need anyone, especially men.

And again, when looking at people in our lives we wonder if that is all it means to be a woman in South Africa today. Can we really be one dimensional and be at peace with that?

As I contemplate these two scenarios and many more I am certain other women can share, I am more convinced that a woman in South Africa in her early 20s battles a lot with less conspicuous everyday struggles – struggles that burden this woman with carrying forward the principles and values of the women who marched heroically to the Union Buildings and those who paved the way in the workplace.

Our struggles are now of identity, definition of who we

are and being comfortable with our choices, whatever they may be.

For me, I have brought it down to choice, which means living truthfully. I choose to be who I want to be, do what I like and define myself anyway I like, and I understand that it is my fundamental right to do so. And on some days those choices are struggles I battle with, but they are my own struggles.

I believe that historically women have been able to assist each other to gain political and economic freedom, but we have not been able to hold onto each other in gaining the freedom of truth. The truth to be who we want to be. The truth that says that, whether we decide to dedicate our lives to our husband and kids or to our career, it is okay. And that, in essence, is what our mothers marched to the Union Buildings for: the right to choose the kind of life they wanted to live for themselves and for future generations to enjoy, without fear of condemnation or judgement.

We need to support each other to be able to live and speak our truth in a safe place, amongst other women. I have realised that, at the core, we all have the same needs, to be understood and validated, and that knowledge can leave us vulnerable. Some of us cover those vulnerabilities in designer clothing and look down on those who cannot afford it, failing to realise that we are all on a journey to discover and live our own unique truths. Failing to understand this has resulted in us perpetuating a cycle of untruths and being inauthentic around each other.

As I write, I am beginning to appreciate the new struggle for truth we as women find ourselves in. I appreciate it because I believe it gives us great opportunities to tell our stories honestly. When I first started believing in my own power and telling another woman my truth, my story, I learnt that I was winning. I learnt I was fearless and was ready for anything. It is only when you are ready to live in truth that you become fearless in speaking it.

What then is my truth?

My truth is that I too have suffered some of the challenges that most if not all South African women face. I will talk specifically about four of them, namely:

- Rape, which I have experienced
- Abuse and violence, both physical and psychological
- Femicide
- Toxic masculinity

Sis Phumzile Mlambo-Ngcuka, South Africa's women's rights advocate at the United Nations (UN), in an article in HuffPost dated 27 March 2017, says violence is the biggest challenge facing women around the world, as progress in gender equality is erratic and at times a baffling contradiction. Some 120 million girls worldwide, roughly one in 10, have experienced forced intercourse or other sexual acts, according to the UN.

Let me now tackle the four topics individually.

Rape

Rape is defined as unlawful sexual intercourse or sexual penetration of the vagina, anus or mouth of another person with or without force by a sex organ, other body part or foreign object *without* the consent of the victim.

As South Africa's women's rights advocate to the UN says, this scourge knows no colour, creed or social class. It happened to me too.

The day I got raped was like any other. Like many other women who have been raped, I will never forget the date. It was 9 August 2012. I'd been dating my partner at the time for more than a year and we had a certain rhythm to our relationship. Prior to this day, we had not been intimate for about two weeks. I was going through some tough challenges and had decided to fast, pray and abstain from sex.

Earlier that day, we'd met and had a tough conversation regarding his finances. We parted and he'd promised he would pass by my house later. I remember distinctly that when the security guard at the gate called to ask if they could open for him, my gut told me to tell him not to, but I ignored it, thinking that it may be rude for me to do so since we had agreed to meet. How I regret not listening to my gut feeling that day. I was also not in the mood to get into an argument with him. Knowing his character, I knew he would badger me with phone calls.

I was already in bed when he arrived, and he decided to watch a football game with my son downstairs. By the time he came to my bedroom, I was almost asleep. He got into my bed and started kissing me. He got aroused and I told him that I was not in the mood. I was premenstrual and my breasts were tender. He did not listen and continued to kiss me while taking my underwear off. He had me pinned down with an arm while doing all of this. I kept asking him to stop but he continued. After he'd penetrated me, he kept telling me to tell him that I would never refuse him again as he continued his sexual assault.

Initially, I was quite stubborn and refused to make such a promise until I saw that he was not going to stop. By this time, I was sobbing uncontrollably and that was when he stopped. He sat by the side of my bed and occasionally tried to calm me down, but each time he tried to touch or advance towards me, I would burst into an avalanche of sobs. I was on the verge of being hysterical. He then asked me what

I wanted him to do and I told him to leave my house. I could have screamed, but the thought of my son finding me in that compromising situation made me shudder. Also, he was much stronger than my son and I feared that Tembela would have wanted to defend me and that he could have been harmed.

The minute he left my room, I jumped up to lock my bedroom door. After he left, I did one thing that rape survivors are not supposed to do; I jumped into the shower to scrub myself raw. I felt so unclean. This was still so surreal. I kept playing the scene over and over in my head and could not make sense of it. He had also seemed angry about something and I kept wondering if it was the conversation we had had earlier.

That night I slept and the following day I called my friend Tembeka to tell her about the ordeal. She came to see me straight away. Meanwhile, my partner had been calling me incessantly but I was not taking his calls. This after I told him on the first call that it was over between us. When I had taken his first call, he had refused to acknowledge that he had raped me, and his retort was that we sometimes have it rough anyway. I explained to him that, rough or not, it was not consensual. He became arrogant and told me that even if I was to go and report it the police at the Sandton police station were his friends and they would not believe me.

It was at this point that I got very angry and hung up on him. I never picked up his calls again after that. In the end I did not report it because there was no longer any evidence and I knew, because of my last name, it was going to be a big rah-rah. One thing I was determined about was that this ordeal was not going to affect my future relationships. I felt that if I allowed him to affect my future relationship with another man, he would still have power over me, and hell would freeze over before I would let such a scum of a man do that to me. I had to claim my power back, and I'm much stronger for it.

A few days later, I told my youngest sister and, a month later, my children. I felt that it was important for my children, especially Pumla, to know about this, for I did not want her, God forbid, if she were to have a similar violent experience, to not talk about it. I believe that as parents if we do not talk about such things, if we do not break the cycle of silence, that cycle will be repeated by our children.

The ordeal that night invoked a repressed memory of a similar attack by an ex-boyfriend in 1984, shortly before the Easter weekend.

An ex-boyfriend I had dated while at Daliwonga High School had come to Clarkebury with a very close friend of mine, Onke. We had been thick as thieves at Daliwonga. Although Onke lived in East London, she had come to visit her relatives in Qumanco, a village outside of Engcobo. After making sure that he would bring me back, I agreed to accompany my ex-boyfriend to drop off Onke in Qumanco. I really did not think anything of it.

On our way back, he kept asking me to take him back and I told him in no uncertain terms that I had moved on. The reason I had ended the relationship was that he had hidden that he was engaged. We must have been about half an hour away from Clarkebury when he pulled off the road to park the car in an isolated spot next to a river. You could not see the road from where he had parked.

He was still trying to convince me to take him back. Again, in my stubbornness, I told him I didn't care what he did to me; I was never going to take him back. He then playfully touched my tummy and asked why it looked like I was pregnant, and I responded cheekily that I was, and the child was my current boyfriend's child. I think this set him off, as the next thing he did was open the cubby hole, pull out a gun and put it against my head. I can still picture it; it was a .38 special. He told me point blank that if I refused to take him back, he would shoot me and dump my body next to the river. I had never been so scared in my entire life. I told him I would take him back and after that he started kissing me and began to rape me. I just lay there, limp, in his car, while he reclined the seat and moved on top of me. I was crying the whole time.

After he was done, he drove me back to Clarkebury and, as he was dropping me off, he told me that he would come and pick me up that same weekend. I can't remember what day it was, but it was during the week. I told my close friend at Clarkebury what happened and told her if he came that she should be the one to go and tell him I was not going with him. I was just too scared of him. This man had put a gun against my head and had had sex with me against my will. I also told Ayanda (the current school principal of Clarkebury), who was friends with my ex. It had been Ayanda who had told him I was at Clarkebury, not knowing what would transpire that night.

I was to discover that his statement about my looking pregnant was true, two weeks later. Although I had missed my menstrual period for about seven weeks, I had put it to my irregular periods rather than pregnancy. I went to a local clinic and they confirmed that I was indeed pregnant.

It is quite bizarre that I had buried this ordeal so deep in my subconscious that it took a similar trauma to bring it to the surface. I hated my ex for bringing this up again, but I suppose it was nature's way for me to deal with both traumas simultaneously.

I did not talk publicly about my 2012 rape until the

#MeToo campaign in 2017. When this campaign started, although I had been following it, I did not think I was going to come out until one morning when I was chatting to one of my male friends.

The conversation started quite innocently when he had sent me a link about a well-known soccer official's alleged raping of a woman, but it was his next comment that set me on a tailspin of anger: What was the lady thinking when she had invited him to her room. I responded by telling him that inviting a person to your suite is not an invitation for rape and further asked him if he knew that a husband can rape his own wife, because, as long as a wife, girlfriend or partner says no and the other person continues, that is rape.

His next response had steam coming out of my ears. He told me it would mean that husbands would have to walk around the house with consent forms. It was then that I told him about my 2012 rape. He was apologetic, but I still took to Facebook to openly talk about my rape for the first time in five years. I was quite surprised by the responses I received, and the stories shared by women on my timeline about their ordeals.

The most peculiar thing about rape is that until you talk or verbalise what has happened it does not exist. For all you know, it may be a figment of your own imagination. Talking about it makes it real.

Rape is a complex subject and we as women are divided in how we view or deal with it. We have the denialists, the matriarchs who are silent about it or who my daughter calls 'the protectors of patriarchy', those who ask why you did not report it or took so long to talk about it and those who use rape for extortion. I will talk about these complex topics individually.

The denialists

This is a group of people who refuse to believe that women can be raped. We saw this in the recent Dros rape incident. I don't think this group of people are really that naïve to think rape does not happen at all. Rather, to them it seems farfetched that a husband or a boyfriend or friend can be responsible for what is called acquaintance rape and that rape is always performed by strangers.

They also believe that a woman saying no is all part of certain bedroom games. How many times have people who have been raped asked themselves the following questions:
- Did I really say no or just shake my head and cry?
- Was it rough sex or was I being violated?
- Did I really consent or was I coerced into submission?

Because rape or any sexual violence happens when a person is at their most vulnerable state, a state of nakedness, this goes to the heart of why it is such a gross violation. Most times, we cover our insecurities and vulnerabilities with clothes. This is the point denialists fail to see.

Denialism by the survivors themselves also exists but it is different from the views of the denialist. This is partly due to the body's automatic response to trauma, coupled with the fear of stigma, and it is compounded if raped by a person you know. Part of you supposes that you may have led them on, which to me is really nonsense. In my view, it is immaterial whether the other party was highly aroused or not, it does not give them the right to sexually assault you.

The protectors of patriarchy – as Pumla puts it

I can never understand why the matriarchs of society – by that I mean the generation a decade or so older than me – do not talk openly about and condemn rape. In many instances, especially if rape is committed by an uncle, stepfather or the like, the survivors are often if not always coerced into not talking about it. The survivor is made to feel guilty that they will bring shame to the family.

As recent as late last year, I received an inbox message that narrated a chilling story of a child who has borne not one but two children by her rapist. The child and her mother still reside in the same house. Why have the elders, both men and women in this family, not reported this to the police? I was made to understand that this girl gave birth to the first child while she was 16, which constitutes statutory rape.

I honestly have not heard condemnation from matriarchs about sexual violence, even on social media.

This will remain a mystery to me. Even in my own family, the matriarchs were very silent. None of them picked up the phone to ask if I was okay or offer any support. That just goes to show how complex the subject matter is.

Why did you not report it?

This is one of the questions that irks me the most, as if reporting it will make it go away or hide that it ever happened.

There are various reasons why women fail to report sexual offences and chief amongst these is that rape survivors are met with scepticism or blame. Questions are asked about what the survivor was wearing or if they were inebriated, as if these are reason enough for any person to be sexually assaulted.

The South African criminal justice system does not have a dedicated and specially trained team to deal with sexual violence crimes. Not only can a trained team know how to handle survivors, they also know how to investigate and prosecute such crimes successfully. Such a team would make it easier for survivors to report these crimes.

During a gender-based violence summit in 2018, I listened to harrowing tales of women who have been brutally raped, some gang raped, and although they had reported their cases, no one had been prosecuted.

Why would any woman want to report it let alone talk about it when successful convictions are very few? Or when society at large asks them why they haven't reported it when they eventually come out, in an effort to unburden themselves and find closure?

I maintain, if you have never been sexually assaulted, you have no right whatsoever to ask a survivor why they took a long time to come out or why they did not report it.

I did not report my rape; does that mean it did not happen or that I asked for it?

Rape should not have a statute of limitations!

Rape used as extortion or accepting payment as compensation

Although the percentage of people who do this is low, it does exist, and we do need to talk about it. I watched in horror recently a video clip showing a young woman boasting about how much power she had over her man, who had apparently disrespected her and called her names. She proceeds to tell whoever she was talking to that since she still has his sperm inside her, she could lay a false charge of rape against him as a way of getting back at him!

This is problematic for me on two fronts. Firstly, and most importantly, it trivialises rape. Sexual assault is not an experience that can be used as power over whoever has done it, but an extremely traumatic experience. It cannot be used to teach somebody a lesson. Secondly, when a person has been sexually assaulted and then entertains payment as compensation it turns it into some sort of transaction. I seriously doubt if there is any person who would want to be paid for being raped, but then people are all different.

How did our grandmothers deal with rape or sexual assault in their time, especially if committed by a family member? There must be some indigenous knowledge somewhere that deals with this.

I strongly believe that as a society we need to dig deep in order to deal with sexual assault cases better.

Abuse and violence against women

Abuse is quite broad in that it includes both emotional and physical abuse. Again, I hear a lot of people asking why a physically abused woman does not leave the relationship. Before I delve into this let me talk about my own emotional abuse.

Pumla's father was emotionally abusive. Around the time I was heavily pregnant with Pumla, he went to a wedding, which he had told me about. My mother and sister happened to attend the same wedding and they both came back livid, as they had seen him with another woman. Mom had never liked him from the beginning and she wasn't shy to tell me.

I chose to stay with him because I was still madly in love with him. To me, there is nothing worse than leaving a person you're still in love with. I did confront him with what Mom and my sister had told me and his retort was that they never liked him anyway. We had been together for over two years and I told him that if my family had that much influence over me, I would have long broken up with him and that the day I terminated the relationship it would be because of my decision to leave not anyone else's.

He was very loving but when he was angry with me he could be extremely emotionally abusive. When I was off, I always spent one or two nights at his townhouse. We would be intimate, and he would sometimes just stop and tell me he could not feel anything. He'd ask me to leave his bed and sleep in the guest room, which I did. This continued even after Pumla was born. He asked me to leave her with him, but he would bring her to me when she wanted to nurse. His emotional abuse was more towards my sexuality, trying to convince me I was not woman enough for him.

After Pumla was born, Mom saw him again with another woman and she could not take it anymore. She came home and told me that since I was refusing to leave him, I must leave her house, as she could not witness this sort of abuse any longer. Mom told me to leave with Pumla, as she was about five months old, but to leave Tembela behind. I packed my things and went to live with him. I knew it was only temporary, as Granddad had bought the Westville house for us by then and we were just waiting for the transfer of the property to move in, which would be in about three weeks.

Although this was going to 'cramp' his philandering ways, he went along with it, as I had chosen him. I had already made up my mind by then that I was going to leave him but wanted to show him that it was because of him not my family. My character is such that once I make up my mind about something, after deliberating and arguing all possible solutions in my head and failing, I leave, permanently, and I never look back.

The emotional abuse continued, as the arrangement was driving him up the wall. He eventually got me a furnished apartment in town which he paid for for two weeks. This was because my sister and I would be moving to our house at the end of the two weeks.

Prior to that, going back to the time we had started dating, he would pick me up and drop me off at St Aidan's and I mistook this as deep caring, but he later told me that nurses lie a lot about their shifts. I realised that this was a form of monitoring my movements. He also did not like me having friends, but this was not a problem. I'm a loner anyway. But it was his insistence that I ask his permission if I wanted to go to town to do shopping so he could take me and bring me back home that bothered me.

This was driving me nuts and I took to not telling him when I was off and wanted to go to town. A week after moving into the apartment he had paid for, a friend of his told him he had seen me in town and, of course, he came running to confront me. In the heat of our argument I told him he did not own me and that he must stop judging me by his own philandering standards. He slapped me and, boy, did I scream.

My neighbour, a white woman, who came rushing to the door when she heard me scream and asked me if she should call the police. That put the fear of God in him, as he begged me not to tell this lady what had happened. Instead I told her that if I needed her I would call her or scream again. I told him if he ever put his hands on me again, he would sleep in a jail cell before he could even blink.

A week later I moved into our house in Westville. After two weeks in our house, he called to tell me he would be coming to pick me up, as he wanted to see his daughter. He knew I always came along, and I told him he could come around seven.

You know how relaxed you are as a woman when you've made up your mind about something, especially terminating a relationship? I was that relaxed when he came.

Usually, when he came, I would be ready and would come out with an overnight bag for Pumla and me. On this night, however, I came out minus her and the overnight bag. He asked me where she was, and I told him she was sleeping and, in any event, even if she was awake, we wouldn't be coming with him, as what we had was over. He started ranting about how he knew we would not last, as my family never liked him. I pointed out to him that I had gone out with him for four years and although my family never liked him, I stayed with him because I wanted the decision to be mine.

I told him he was welcome to see and visit his daughter, but it had to be during the day, as she was not old enough to stay at his place alone overnight.

And just like that, our relationship was over. Although there were remnants of love, I left because when I had looked at myself in the mirror, I could not recognise myself. Gone was the Ndileka who was carefree and full of life. I lived with my sister, but we could not laugh as we used to. I had been free spirited but that was gone, and I was isolated from my family. The slapping incident had been the last straw for me.

Although my abuse was not as severe as most, I am giving you this background to illustrate how abusers chip away at your self-esteem slowly and systematically. Fortunately for me, I was born with gallons of self-esteem and have a strong sense of self that was instilled in me by my mom and both my grandmothers. Most women are not so fortunate. I came out barely scathed, but I was bruised alright, as I stayed single for about five years before getting into another romantic relationship. I just wanted to raise my children in peace.

People looking in from the outside are very quick to judge women who stay in abusive relationships, but until you are in such a relationship, you cannot fully grasp what these women are confronted with daily.

Let me briefly explain the cycle of abuse and why people stay in abusive relationships.

Why do people stay in abusive relationships?

I have heard this question a lot, especially recently, as domestic violence is getting more and more exposed. Some are downright harsh as to go on and say that they have no sympathies for people who stay in abusive relationships.

The thing is that when it comes to abusive relationships, it's never easy to just leave. Society normalises unhealthy behaviour. People may not understand that their relationship is abusive. Society gives many reasons for why a person is abusive, ranging from growing up in an abusive environment to perhaps watching parents being abusive to one another. I feel that these reasons are used as excuses. To demonstrate the extent to which society has normalised unhealthy behaviour, I will bring up the incident that happened a day after Babes Wodumo's abuse by her boyfriend went viral.

After posting on my Facebook timeline that I was on Babes's side, a guy friend sent me this message: 'Some few points we need to note about #Babes-Mampintsha saga is that:

1. These are two young persons who are in a LOVE RELATIONSHIP.
2. They happen to have a misunderstanding (which is common in many young relationships in particular & relationships in general).
3. They are unfortunate to have both been celebrities.

Let us therefore assist them to reconcile than try to destroy their relationship. A breakup is not a solution.'

Suffice it to say, I really went off on him.

If you have been in an abusive relationship before, it is often easy to see the signs a mile away. I was able to spot abusive tendencies in a relationship I was in in late 2016 and early 2017, and thank the Lord I ended it quickly. A month after I started dating him, I had spent the night at his house and was getting ready to leave. He was in the bathroom dressing. He came into the room and started going off at me about a friend I have on Facebook who had supposedly 'stolen' his pose – the pose was of this gentleman sitting on a chair in the gym lifting a heavy dumbbell. According to him, he was the only person in the entire universe to have a pose like that. I honestly wanted to laugh so much as this was the most preposterous thing I have ever heard, until I saw that he was dead serious.

It was what he said that was cause for concern, as he told me that he hoped I did not embarrass him, and when I asked him what he meant, he did not explain further. I let that slide, putting it to some pressure he was facing at the time.

The next incident was when I had driven to his house after he told me he would be there. I had to wait in the car for an hour before he came back. When I asked him why he did not tell me he was running that late after giving him a lot of scowls to register my annoyance, he turned around and said I was not even asking him if he was fine. I really found that funny and told him that since he was in front of me, he was obviously fine. He did not find my amusement laughable.

The day I decided to terminate the relationship was the night we were having a debate about religion. He was a member of a charismatic church. Our debate was around fasting and whether partners could be intimate during the fasting period and what a person may do during fasting. His belief was that if fasting is to be effective, one needs to abstain from sex and not eat or drink until after 6 pm for the duration of the fast, as per his 'pastor's' teachings.

I told him that first and foremost, spiritual relationships are sacred contracts between individuals and God and that no human being can tell me my relationship with Him should be this or that. Furthermore, fasting should be done according to what you decide. I may elect to fast from food and not water or do a dry fast or a half day fast. This got him into such a tense state that he told me I was going to weaken him spiritually because of my beliefs. That, to me, raised red flags. I have experienced how abusers box you into their belief system slowly and steadily.

The following day, I called him and told him it was best to go our separate ways, as we had completely opposite ideas about a lot of things. The reason I broke up with him over the phone was that after our first major disagreement, I had gone to his house to get clothes I had left there, and he pulled a fast one on me. After loading my stuff in the boot, he asked me to take him to the nearest filling station to get an airtime voucher. Like an idiot, I agreed.

When we got back, I wanted to drop him off outside his complex and make a U-turn, but because it was drizzling slightly, he asked me to drop him off next to his house. When we got there, he would not get out of the car and said we must go next to the gate, as he still had to load his airtime and it would be easier to open the gate from there.

By now I was getting really agitated because it was late, well after 10:30 pm, and Pumla was eight months pregnant and approaching her delivery date, and he was aware of that. I was also annoyed and this is why I wanted to drop him off at the gate in the first place. When we reached the gate, he refused to open it. He started trying to convince me how he was good for me and all sorts of nonsense. We were in the car for almost an hour and I had to switch the ignition off.

It was getting late and I could see he was not going to open the gate, so I convinced him that I would leave my clothes at his house to appease him, that we were going talk about things. He was to learn about my passive aggressive personality the next day, as I blocked him from my phone. He then bought another SIM card to reach out to me and that was when I told him I was not the woman for him. He could argue a person into exhaustion and submission, which is why I ended the relationship via a text message. I knew the signs of emotional abuse enough to recognise that he was the worst kind of emotional abuser.

Oh! Did I tell you that after I had shaved my hair off, he instructed me to keep a clean-shaven head by shaving daily because the grey hair made me look so old!

So, trust me when I say, if you recognise signs of abuse of any kind in a relationship, run and run fast because abuse can ultimately lead to death, which is another topic I want to briefly talk about.

Femicide

When I found out that the femicide rate in our country is five times more than the global rate, I was speechless for a moment until I remembered 2017. On almost every social media post, women from various parts of the country were reported missing only to be found brutally murdered and most, if not all, had been raped.

According to an article on femicide in South Africa on Africacheck.org, between April and December 2016, the police recorded a total of 14 333 murders and of these 1713 victims were women. This translates to a woman being murdered every four hours. It's mind boggling. This year alone we have seen several brutal murders of women by their partners, with other cases coming to the fore, which begs the question, why do these men resort to killing their partners?

In a 2018 article in *Times Live* titled 'Femicide in South Africa: Why men kill', Javu Baloyi, spokesperson for the Commission for Gender Equity, said men kill women mostly because they fail to navigate their way around rejection. Among the key reasons they do this is an embedded complex that many men suffer from. (I really must research where this comes from, this complex, a little further.)

Javu Baloyi, speaking on the 'curse of the ex', a trend where women are killed by their ex-lovers, said that men don't understand that they need to let go when there is no longer love in a relationship because they think they own women.

Most men cannot handle rejection and some turn to abuse, at times murder, when rejection becomes too much to handle.

Toxic masculinity and femicide

I want to talk about these two topics simultaneously, as I believe they are interlinked. While writing this book, I had to do a lot of research pertaining to femicide and why some men end up killing their partners, exes and spouses. Among the articles I stumbled across, one article that made sense to me was titled 'Toxic Masculinity and Violence in South Africa'. The research was also driven by incidences of gender violence and the killing of women in 2017.

In the article, a lot of research has been done into men, masculinities and violence. This is because notions of masculinity and what it means to be a man seem to be the driving factors behind much of the risky behaviour some men engage in. I just feel some men feel women are their property. In a recent conversation over social media with a man, I found that men often have chauvinistic notions towards women. This conversation emanated from a post I had about women dying with protection orders in their handbags. This man's response to my comment was that many casualties could be avoided if women kept their mouths shut during arguments. To say I was shocked is an understatement. This to me implies that even if a man is degrading and disrespecting you as a woman, you ought to keep your mouth shut to avoid being abused. That is not love but control.

I have come across this type of man in my lifetime, a man who feels his word must not be challenged. An example of this is an ex-partner of mine who felt I was weakening him spiritually simply because I challenged his beliefs on fasting. In conversation once, I told him I was fasting and he dismissed me because in his view fasting meant not eating or drinking whereas to me it meant not eating but drinking fluids. He often wanted me to dress in a certain way and have my hair in a certain way. However, because I had been in an emotionally abusive relationship before I recognised the signs early, I ended the relationship.

I recently had a discussion with my younger sister, Zinhle, about the definition of toxic masculinity. She argued that by using 'toxic' as a prefix to 'masculinity' it is disempowering to men who are Alpha males, in as far as we both understood an Alpha male to be one who is a provider and a protector. She went on to explain that the term toxic masculinity is tantamount to saying 'bitchy feminists'.

After my discussion with my sister I now believe toxic masculinity is where all the norms of masculinity are seen as violent, unemotional and sexually aggressive and have a harmful impact on society and the individual.

In my Xhosa culture I believe toxic masculinity rears its ugly head when men go to initiation school, as their behaviour changes most of the time after they come out. This I noticed in my own son, who, after coming back from initiation school, suddenly refused to do chores that he did before he went, claiming he was now a 'man'. I quickly stamped it out by telling him he was not a man in my house, and my stance killed the patriarchical attitude right there and then. Often when this attitude goes unchecked, it results in hyper-masculinity.

I have asked men in my family and my friends by and large what is taught at initiation schools, as it seems to me that for most Xhosa men, this is where hyper-masculinity and patriarchy become entrenched. My questions have been met with scoff and abrupt dismissal because I am a woman. Even Tembela point blank refused to tell me what they are taught. One time when I asked this over one of the social media platforms, some men called me names.

Boys have been raised to believe that they should not be reprimanded for wrongdoing and that they must rarely take responsibility for their actions. From a young age, children are taught that girls should 'act like a lady' and if boys do something wrong, it is shrugged off with words like 'boys will be boys'. One would have thought this would change in this century, but it has become more entrenched. However, it is not only in schools and at home where boys are socialised to believe in their own superiority; this message is being delivered through peer pressure, the media, military influences, as well as political influences, which all lead to the view that violence is an acceptable behaviour in men.

Positive masculinity is something humanity in all its structures, civil society, organised labour, LGBTQ groups, government, business and citizens have to start putting at the top of the agenda when it comes to dealing with domestic violence in all its forms.

Men should be at the front, middle, back and side of this dialogue, for if we are to rid society of the scourge of domestic violence, men have got to be part of these conversations.

Chapter 16

The caregiver

THE NOTION THAT CHILDREN LEARN by emulation happens to be true in my case. I guess since Rundu was a community nurse, it was no surprise that I chose nursing as my career. Or, did it choose me?

I know that when I started nursing it came easily to me. I can safely say that I cruised through my training as a general nurse and midwife.

The challenge of being the nurse in the family is that you become the resident family nurse. My sister Nandi, who at some point was working in the United States, would call me to find out what medication she should take for most of her ailments. Even after I left mainstream nursing, I continued to be the 'resident family nurse'. But this soon became a problem.

When Mom took her own life, I truly blamed myself for not having seen the signs. I mean I did psychiatry during my years of training as a nurse; I should have realised the signs. I should have realised that her moods, switching from euphoria to depression, were bordering on dangerous, and for the longest time I blamed myself, until my therapy years.

During the time Rundu was ill, my career was not so much a problem, because her illness did not last very long. I remember that when one of my cousins, Thandi, called the morning of 29 April 2004 to tell me that I had to come to Milpark Hospital, as Rundu was highly confused, I rushed to see her. Since I had seen her the previous day and she had been fine, I put the confusion down to perhaps a drug that is usually given to elderly patients to help them sleep called Ativan, whose side effects are confusion in this age group.

Upon my arrival at the hospital, I took one look at her and immediately knew the die was cast. This was to be one of the times I hated being a nurse. Ignorance is sometimes bliss, especially when your close family is in a healthcare facility. I had to call those family members who could make it to come and say their last goodbyes, as I knew it was a matter of time before she departed. How do you tell aunts, cousins and sisters alike that you know the imminent is about to happen? In these instances, the nurse in me kicks in and the family member disappears. The danger in this is that I could not go through the emotions of processing what was happening, and the situation was to repeat itself again, first Uncle Kgatho got ill and then Granddad.

I mentioned earlier that when my aunt told me about Uncle Kgatho's cholecystectomy operation my heart fell, as I had seen very few patients survive this operation during my years working in the ICU. During his illness I became more like a family nurse consultant and had to explain most of the procedures done to him and the medication given. There was a time when he was on a dopamine drip and adrenalin infusion at the same time to regulate both his blood pressure and heart by titrating one against the other. While I knew why this was being done, it was sometimes difficult to explain all of this to my family. At times, I just did not want to deal with it.

As a nurse I can decipher doctor's notes and read charts, heart monitors, ventilators, you name it, and know exactly what is happening. I also know that as a health practitioner there are limits to what you are allowed to tell the relatives without overstepping your boundaries as a nurse. I found myself conflicted, as I was both a health practitioner and a family member. Again, as most of my family members were processing his illness, I was being a nurse and could not process any of my emotions.

In order to become an effective nurse, you have to dial down your compassion, not in the sense that you become callous, so that you can carry off your duties successfully. Imagine if nurses became attached to every patient they treated. If that patient died, they would be very distraught, and it would affect their ability to do their jobs. As a nurse you have to strike a fine balance between being compassionate and being detached.

The dilemma I was faced with was in not knowing when my duties as a family member and that of a health professional started and ended. How much can I tell my relatives? How brutally honest can I be with them?

Nurses are bound by a code of conduct called the Nightingale Pledge, which goes like this:

> *I solemnly pledge myself before God and in the presence of this assembly to pass my life in purity and to practice my profession faithfully. I will abstain from what is deleterious and mischievous and will not take or knowingly administer any harmful drug. I will do all in my power to maintain and elevate the standard of my profession and will hold in confidence*

> *all personal matters committed to my keeping and family affairs coming to my knowledge in the practice of my calling. With loyalty, I will aid the physician in his work, and as a missioner of health, I will dedicate myself to devoted service for human welfare.*

Reading this pledge, it's easy to see why I was conflicted.

If this conflict was challenging with Uncle Kgatho, it was compounded with Granddad. With him my caregiving status started when he got ill in January 2011. Since I had decided to take a sabbatical, from then on I spent the bulk of my time keeping him company. My life revolved around him, literally, and it is something I will never regret, as it brought us closer together.

When he was admitted to hospital in June 2013, things got more complicated for me. I could not separate the nurse from the grandchild, which put me and the medical team on a collision course at times. For instance, I knew how toxic some of the antibiotics were, albeit being crucial for the treatment of his infections, and would argue the necessity of putting him on such drugs. At times I realised that it was not the nurse arguing but the grandchild, which was unfair. I struggled with this balance.

Things came to a head one morning when we had our usual meeting and briefing with his medical team. I formed part of this team, owing to my experience as an ICU nurse. The team was explaining the necessity of keeping Granddad on a vasoconstrictor – medication aimed at constricting the blood vessels – which was having extreme side effects. Now I knew that it was important for him to be on this medication, but I was highly frustrated and worried. I proceeded to ask the head physician in the team that, were this his father or grandfather, would he do the same?

Even I knew this was below the belt, especially as a health

professional. It was something that I regretted then and still do. Granddad's medical team wanted the best for him and were under the scrutiny of the entire world should anything happen to him. The physician got extremely upset with this question and the meeting ended on a somewhat sour note, but, because we all wanted what was best for him, we had to smoke the peace pipe the very next day. At the precise moment I had asked this question, the lines between caregiver and grandchild became very blurred.

Then there were also times when the medical team were not forthcoming with information, for reasons I understood. At these times I would often get calls from my relatives asking me to level with them, and again I was conflicted. The medical team was always forthright with me, due to the respect we gave each another as health professionals, but how was I to divulge details to my family without betraying their trust?

There were also times the team relied on me to reign in the family, especially when it came to visiting hours. Here again, the lines were often blurred.

As challenging as these times were, I would not trade them for anything. I felt duty bound to make the sacrifices I did, as it was something that had been done for thousands of years in African families – caring for your loved ones, especially the old and infirm.

Nowadays this caring is called 'black tax', a concept I'm still battling to come to terms with.

From conversations I have gleaned that this term has a negative connotation, and, in my view, it is alien in the African culture. It implies that one has a noose around their neck to take care of those who come after them, or to take care of family members who are old and infirm. When did taking care of family become a burden? This compassion Africans have for family and each other is what makes us unique and is called '*ubuntu*' or humanity.

Part Five

Chapter 17

Finding my voice

FINDING MY VOICE IN MY FAMILY was very difficult. Firstly, I have a hierarchical family where the generation that precedes mine can be extremely bossy. Not only that, I come from a generation where I have to respect my elders no matter what. I may be the eldest in the next generation, but I had to toe the line for the bulk of my adult life.

I really struggled. For instance, after finishing nursing school, having a professional qualification under my belt, I thought of being a fashion model, but my family would not hear of it. I ended up doing nursing, although I did grow to love it.

Finding my voice has been a long journey. When I left nursing, I went over to the marketing side of nursing and worked for Prime Cure Clinic. After about four years with them, I left and joined the medical aid field as a business development manager. After two years with this medical aid company, I left the medical field totally and joined a recruitment company, again as a business development manager in the public sector.

It was while at this recruitment company that I got roped into working for a company that was looking for a woman to join them in acquiring a coal mine in Witbank. We started immediately with a prospecting licence application, but 18 months into the process we hit a snag. There were two members in the group who did not see eye to eye. If they were in a room together, sparks would fly. After a lot of trying to manage the personality clashes between the two, to no avail, it became clear that we had reached a stalemate.

After much discussion, we decided to sell the mine and, because we had to sell before the prospecting licence had been granted, we sold it at a loss.

Now I was back home with no company and no job. One night when I was speaking to a friend of mine, Xola, he told me that a mutual friend of ours could assist me with a job and proceeded to give me his number. I called Moss at Equiton and he asked me to come to his office the next day.

After he explained what the job would entail, he hired me on the spot as a project coordinator for an RDP housing project in Rietvallei. The pay was really good.

When I started working with Equiton, I knew nothing about the construction industry and had to learn fast. I enjoyed what I did.

My job entailed everything from interrogating the bill of quantities for a house, making sure the contractors were not overcharging, allocating stands to contractors, to liaising with the quantity surveyor (QS) to come and do inspections of each stage of constructing a 40-square-metre RDP house. These inspections were carried through from the foundation stage, to wall plating, laying roof trusses, roof construction, to snagging, until the house was without snags and could be handed over.

Finding my voice

Now, Rietvallei was what is called a brownfield construction in that there were houses on the stands prior to construction. Because there had been a delay in the construction of their houses, the residents of Rietvallei had built shacks on their allocated stands. The construction of these 2 300 RDP houses was part of rectifying this. These shacks had to be removed from the centre of the plot, and the quantity surveyor had to first peg them.

This is where I learnt the pitfalls of a brownfield construction project. There was a lot of theft of building materials by the community, to the extent that we had to have a 24-hour security guard at the construction site where all the building materials were kept. There was also theft of window handles and we later learnt that, since they were made of brass, people were melting them and selling them.

The other challenge came from the construction companies themselves. Moss had made it compulsory for us to choose small construction companies to give them a chance to prove themselves. These construction companies had to get their labour from the community. The challenge arose because some contractors wanted to cut corners. There had to be Brickforce to bind the bricks together to avoid structural cracks on certain levels on the wall plate. Some contractors would skip some levels, resulting in the wall being demolished, as they could not pass the inspection.

This project was meant to take 18 months but, because of delays due to the rainy season and challenges of constructing in a brownfields project, we took three years to complete all 2 300 houses.

I learnt so much about the construction industry when I worked for Equiton that I think I could supervise the construction of my own house if the need ever arose.

After leaving Equiton, I had to redefine myself and find

my voice again. That voice is now expressed through my foundation, the Thembekile Mandela Foundation, and the various programmes espoused by the foundation.

Social media has also provided me with the opportunity to make my voice more heard and, trust me, it has not been easy. The tendency is always to be compared to my grandfather, which can be annoying at the best of times. No more is this evident than when I post about politics or respond to comments. There is a general trend of thinking that because I did not go into exile or was not in the streets fighting the apartheid system, I therefore do not have a voice. People go as far as asking me if I go door-to-door campaigning, to which I respond that my vote gives me the right to hold the political party I voted for to account.

Some comments become personal and proclaim that I'm not even related to my grandfather. Some ask why I am using my surname, to which I retort and ask which surname I should be using, as I'm born of Nelson Mandela's firstborn and not just his firstborn but his eldest son. Although this can be exhausting, nowadays I choose not to engage in such conversations questioning my heritage.

The foundation has by far allowed my voice to be heard more loudly and clearly. Previously, I was referred to as Ndileka Mandela, eldest grandchild of Nelson Mandela. Nowadays I'm referred to as the founder of the Thembekile Mandela Foundation.

You have no idea how liberating that is. I am slowly but surely escaping from the shadow of my grandfather. I now get invited to express my views on myriad topics, not because of my last name, but because of my stance and because of my voice. It is finally being heard.

Chapter 18

Finding my passion

FINDING MY PASSION BEGAN IN 2012 when I received a call from a family friend asking me to take Clarkebury on as a project. He told me that Clarkebury Senior Secondary School (formerly a teacher's training college), a school that not only Granddad attended, but I did too, was in a state of disrepair and that I needed to do something for it. He had wanted me to come to the school on 18 July 2012. I explained to him that I already had a project for my 67 minutes. I also want to spend the day with Granddad, as this was tradition. At that time Granddad was ailing, and I wanted to spend whatever time I could with him.

We, however, reached a compromise that I would make time to come to Clarkebury at another point in the month of July. After our conversation, I called a journalist friend of mine, Sophie Mokoena, and asked if she knew any businesspeople who could accompany me to the school on a fact-finding mission. She told me she had a person in mind and that we just needed to go and see him. Sophie made all the arrangements for the meeting and we went together to see Mr Tim Tebeile, who explained to us that, although his company had already identified a project for Mandela Day, he was interested in paying Clarkebury a visit.

Around 23 July 2012, we took a plane chartered by Tim to Mthatha and drove to Clarkebury. We found that the school's boarding house, where I used to be a boarder, was in complete disrepair. Adjacent to this boarding house was another one that looked fairly new, but it was also in a state of dilapidation. The school principal, Ayanda Matshayana, explained that when Clarkebury ceased to be a teacher training college, when Minister Kader Asmal did away with teacher training colleges, the boarding houses had remained empty and were later vandalised. The one I used to stay in had caught fire at some point.

Ayanda explained to us that, prior to him being the principal, the school had extremely poor matric results – the pass rate was 38%. Ayanda, who was also a product of Clarkebury, was then asked to come and assist. It had been about three years since he had become the principal when the results started to improve. The year before we spoke, they had been slightly above 60%. He had done this through serious dedication, by weeding out the rogue elements – students who were smoking weed at school and being delinquents – getting the parents and the SGB very involved and asking his team of teachers to put in extra work. As a result of all his interventions and the results improving year on year, they had received an influx of students, some who had to walk long distances to school.

Since about 60% were girl learners, this walking exposed them to being raped if they were walking home late. He gave us this background to make us understand why these boarding houses needed to be fixed. Both buildings were

Finding my passion

still solid and all they needed were plumbing, sewerage, carpentry and electricity.

He also took us around the school premises. The older classrooms, including Granddad's classroom, had been converted into a multi-purpose centre, with a sewing room and a woodwork room. Granddad's classroom had been converted into a science laboratory. All these classrooms had not a single piece of equipment in them and that was another reason Ayanda had wanted me to come.

Since we had gone on this trip with the South African Bureau of Standards (SABS), they jumped at the opportunity of kitting it out with state-of-the-art science laboratory equipment, and they delivered on their promise by handing over the equipment to Ayanda and his team in 2014. We also undertook fundraising for the repair and refurbishment of the boarding house.

On that day, 26 July 2012, the seed for the Thembekile Mandela Foundation (TMF) was planted, and I haven't looked back since.

After my career in nursing and the medical field, I had not made up my mind about what I wanted to do with my life. I just knew I never wanted to be working for someone else. I discussed with Granddad continuing his legacy of rural upliftment and he approved. When he had started the Nelson Mandela Foundation (NMF), Granddad raised funds for the construction of proper schools in the rural areas of both Limpopo and Eastern Cape. These two provinces have the largest number of mud schools. The two pillars of the NMF were health and education. In education it was mainly the eradication of mud schools and in health the NMF was mainly doing HIV/AIDS advocacy work.

Prior to 2012, the NMF had rebranded and became the Nelson Mandela Centre of Memory, a digital archive repository of the life and times of Nelson Mandela and other struggle icons. Since the rebranding, these health and education programmes were discontinued, and I felt that, through the TMF, I could continue where he had left off, albeit with a different approach to these issues. He gave it his blessing and I set the ball rolling with attempts to register the TMF. However, due to his serious ill health later that year and the whole of 2013, which kept my hands full, I was unable to until February 2014, two months after his funeral.

The registration itself happened in a peculiar way. On the morning of 11 February 2014, I was doing a *Morning Live* interview about Granddad's release. Two weeks before that, I had received a call from Ayanda in Clarkebury sharing with me the great news that their matric students had received a 94% pass rate and that 30 of these students had received university entrance passes. Clarkebury had moved from a 38% matric pass rate to a 94% pass rate in three years. Ayanda, being Ayanda, asked me to come and attend their celebrations of this phenomenal achievement but to not come empty-handed.

The celebrations were in a week's time. I called a friend of mine who worked for Samsung to donate 30 tablets to the students who had achieved university entrance passes. To my surprise, the CEO of Samsung agreed but the tablets were to be dispatched at a later date to Clarkebury. I went to attend the celebrations and shared the news with the staff, students and student governing body of Clarkebury. SABC's Zimkhita Manqinana interviewed me after these celebrations and arranged a follow-up interview with *Morning Live* back in Johannesburg.

Towards the end of the *Morning Live* interview, Leanne Manas asked me about what I was doing at Clarkebury and how people who wanted to assist could do so. I told her it had always been my intention to register an entity but had been unable to for reasons I have already stated. Unbeknownst to me, a person I had met a year earlier at the Muldersdrift Heia Safari Ranch by the name of Myles Zengeya was watching that morning.

Myles called straight after my interview and asked to meet with me. I met with him and the owners of the company he was working for a few days later. They expressed interest in assisting me with the registration of the foundation. Myles did all the work, drafted the constitution, filled in the form from the Department of Social Development and, by the end of February, the Thembekile Mandela Foundation was a fully fledged registered non-governmental organisation.

Before launching the foundation, I visited Mom Graça to tell her the news. I will never forget what she said to me. She said, 'Darling, thank you for bringing Thembi back to the present. You have given him a face. Up until now, Thembi was stuck in childhood as images of him are that of a young boy.' I had never thought of it that way before, that Dad had been a faceless person in the Mandela family. Sure, he is mentioned in most books written about Granddad, but he had remained a child. Very few people knew he had married and had two girls before he died.

On 24 February 2014, 45 years after Dad died, I, Ndileka Mandela, his eldest child, held a media launch in Houghton, two months after I had buried my grandfather. I had come full circle and it felt great.

Mom Graça's comment made me more determined to keep Dad's memory alive by continuing what Granddad had started with the NMF. It would be months before the foundation was fully functional. Most people who start foundations have some funds to kickstart. I had zero funds. I had not been working since September 2010.

Fast forward to April 2013 when I had to attend the 21st birthday celebrations of a close friend of my daughter's at the Vaal. The day after the birthday, when I went for breakfast, I was told to wait a bit, as the hotel restaurant was full, but Pumla's friend's father told me I could go and sit with Nikky, the birthday girl's mother, as there was a place at their table. At this table I met one of Nikky's relatives, Kenny Boshego, who had worked at the NMF and was in charge of education before the programmes were discontinued. I just could not believe how fortuitous this meeting was.

I asked her if she could join the foundation as a board member. She refused and told me she would rather be in the operations division. I told her I had no money to pay salaries and she told me we could just start, God would provide. I told her I was to travel to Tennessee upon a friend's invitation to see what inroads I could make. She told me that it was fine and, when I came back, we could start.

Prior to that, Myles had managed to get us office space that Regiments, a company based in Johannesburg, was to sponsor for two years. It was located in Central Street in Houghton.

On 3 May 2014, both Kenny Boshego and I converged at our new offices. I had been under the impression that the office came with office furniture, but that was not the case. Kenny was not worried one bit. She said she had office furniture at home and had it brought the following day. Two days later, we both started, armed with our laptops and cell phones. Kenny still had some contacts she worked with when she was with the Nelson Mandela Foundation and proceeded to call them for support.

While waiting for funds to start coming in, we sat and discussed what the TMF should focus on, as we knew that the focus had to be a little different from the original way

Granddad had intended. We settled on education, health and youth development. The programmes were to run as follows:

- Health – Pride of the Rural Girl (more on this later)
- Education – focus on infrastructure requirements: computer laboratories, science laboratories and libraries, in short, leverage on the fourth industrial revolution
- Youth development – empowering unemployed youth

All of this was to be done in rural areas. Since I grew up in the rural areas, I know that there are gifted children who, because of the lack of amenities, cannot and do not make it and it was imperative for us to concentrate on that sector. We elected to concentrate on adolescent children because we felt that there were already a lot of NGOs that tackle early childhood development. I personally know that there are two crucial stages in a child's developmental life and that is early childhood and the adolescent stage.

In my view, early childhood is the first catchment area for a child's development and the next one is adolescence. If the development of a child cannot be rectified at adolescent stage, that child is lost forever. That is why we chose to focus on this area.

But, first things first, the foundation needed funds. Dr Liaqat Azam came through for the foundation with flying colours. I had met him a few years earlier when sis Bongi Mkhabela had taken me with her to a meeting when she was looking for donations for the Nelson Mandela Children's Hospital. We struck up a friendship and have been friends ever since. He became head of resource mobilisation at the foundation.

Two weeks after we started operations at the foundation,

Liaqat arranged a meeting with Rizwan Adatia, a renowned philanthropist based in Maputo. Rizwan loved what we wanted to do and pledged R600k on the spot to be paid in three tranches. I was in utter disbelief; we had opened a bank account three days prior to this meeting. True to his word, Rizwan had the funds transferred.

Mandela Day 2014 was fast approaching, and we discussed what we could do in order to gain visibility and attract some funding. While still toying around with ideas, a lady who was producing sanitary pads visited our office. It was what she shared with us that was an eye opener and resulted in Pride of the Rural Girl, which became our flagship programme. She showed us a study that showcased that up to three million girls in southern Africa do not go to school because of a lack of pads.

I was shocked by this to say the least. I never thought that in the 21st century there would be a girl learner that could not attend school due to this. I learnt that, rather than bleed through their dresses and face ridicule, they opted to not go to school. Some of them used toilet paper or newspapers.

We were to form a partnership with this woman since she was running her own packaging company. She told us she was buying her pads from China. The only snag was that she wanted us to buy from her and we did not have funds. One of our members on the advisory board suggested that we host a breakfast to raise funds for the programme.

Since there was very little time for us to do anything for Mandela Day, we put our efforts into hosting the breakfast and settled on a date of 8 August 2014 at the Maslow Hotel. While busy with this fundraiser, we started to look for a local manufacturer who could sell to us at cost and found one just outside Johannesburg.

We organised this event ourselves with a few volunteers.

Finding my passion

Mama Graça gave a very moving keynote address and the event itself was a success, as we found a partner, the Westonaria Community Trust (WCT), which sponsored 6 382 girls for the sanitary pads programme. With the other funds raised at the breakfast, we were able to support 10 000 girls in total in Gauteng, Mpumalanga and the Eastern Cape. All 10 000 girls received a supply of sanitary pads for a whole year. We came up with the name Pride of the Rural Girl, as we were restoring their pride lost through using unsanitary substances for their periods and bleeding through their uniforms.

Since we believe in sustainable programmes, our intention was to supply the sanitary pads for a period of five years. We came to the five-year cycle for the simple reason that if one girl learner loses up to 50 days of schooling a year in a five-year cycle from Grade Eight to Grade 12, each will have lost a whole year of schooling. A whole year of missing schoolwork is a lot and no consideration is given to these girls when they sit for their final senior examinations.

This project is close to my heart because I view the gesture of providing sanitary towels as a contribution our generation can give to these girls to allow them to exercise their fundamental right to education. This right is a choice that should never be taken away from them because of circumstances beyond their control.

2015 and 2016 were good years for us as a foundation, as we were able to make an impact in a short space of time. 2016 saw us embarking on an agricultural entrepreneurship programme. This project was funded by the Mining Qualifications Authority (MQA). All mines pay a levy to MQA and these funds have to be ploughed back in the areas where they mine. Together with WCT we selected unemployed youth who were then trained in agricultural practices. The project commenced in March 2017 and was completed in November of the same year.

Since starting the Thembekile Mandela Foundation I have been working tirelessly to continue the legacy of my grandfather. The foundation has become a true parent to me. It is showing me the beauty of being good to others, especially women and girls in rural areas. It is my parent because it teaches me to sit with a woman in a village and know that despite our different social conditions and locations, her struggles are my struggles and she deserves my respect and love. The foundation has made me empathetic enough to feel the pain of others so that I cannot help but take it upon myself to help them and find solutions. It truly is my parent because it corrects me many times, to ensure I keep on a path of authenticity and not judge others, as I am neither different nor special from them.

The foundation has also become a parent in the way it teaches me every day how challenging non-governmental work can be. It is the work of the heart. Many people who see me on the news launching one project after the next, be it giving books or shoes to school children, may think it is a piece of cake. Foundation work can be gut wrenching, as I have to say no to many worthwhile causes due to a lack of funding. People often think that because of my last name I can walk into any company and they will give me a blank cheque to utilise for any of the programmes the foundation espouses. Far from it.

I remember early in 2017 I had taken pictures of me giving school shoes to various schools in the West Rand and posted them on my Facebook timeline. I was inundated with requests from friends in various schools to donate to their schools as well. Little did they know that what looks so easy and perhaps beautiful in pictures was difficult work that took almost a year to pull off.

What compounds the difficulties that most non-profit organisations face, especially here at home, is that in 2015, South Africa was deemed a middle-income country (MIC). This is a ranking by the World Bank. MIC countries are nations with a per capita gross national income (GNI) of between $1 005 and $12 235 (R13 969 and R170 065 depending on the exchange rate at the time). As a result of this declaration, it has become difficult to attract, specifically, foreign funding.

Coupled with this, there are challenges facing non-profit organisations globally and the TMF is not immune to these. Some of these challenges include:

- Shrinking assistance from government: Many NPOs depend on government assistance, which may be in the form of grants. Shrinking budgets at state, national, provincial and municipal levels mean there is less to go around. Most NPOs end up getting less than they are used to and some get nothing. We have certainly seen this here at home. The Total Shutdown movement that was promised some funding at the gender summit last year did not receive any funding.
- Stable income and accurate budgeting: This I can attest to. Having a steady income from any source is hard for NPOs. Donor funds may be unsteady throughout the year or stop altogether, rendering it hard to do any budgeting. The focus of the organisation then moves to securing enough to cover overheads before seeing what is left for projects.
- Not being run like a business: With much emphasis on performance, an NPO may struggle with remembering that it is still a business that must have a positive bottom line. NPOs often put their local goals

at the forefront and their business objectives second, which may be fine, until there is not enough coming in to cover what is going out.
- Attracting the right staff with limited resources: When money is tight, an NPO may be able to attract people who believe in its cause, but they may not be top talents in their fields. It is difficult to justify a large salary or a benefit package at an NPO, and that leads to the best and brightest talent looking elsewhere.
- Increase in need for services: Across the board, NPOs are seeing an increase in the need for services as poverty escalates and many more people are facing economic hardships.
- Growth is risky: Even if your NPO is attracting enough funding to serve all the people it wants and attracting the right talent, growth can be precarious, as funding is not guaranteed and the staff is often not contracted to stay, thus making putting money into growth risky.

These are some of the challenges the TMF has come across, but I keep on going on. You may ask why? I do this because:
- It bothers me that, in a world of abundance, there are still people who go to bed without food.
- It bothers me that there are girl learners who miss school because of a lack of sanitary wear.
- It bothers me that, during the fourth industrial revolution, our National Department of Basic Education has failed to leverage on the technology available to make it possible for science and maths teachers to teach thousands of learners in real time via Smart Boards and Wi-Fi.
- It bothers me that there are still school children dying

in pit latrines in rural schools when there is technology available that can turn excrement into powder.

I do my NGO work for the sheer love of it. I will never forget the experience I had when the foundation went to its first drop-off of sanitary wear in Marapyane, Mpumalanga. The experience humbled me. I saw girls literally crying upon receiving their packs. The joy in their faces was priceless and it made me vow to dedicate myself to finding solutions to assist in whatever way I can.

Although as a foundation we hit a snag in 2017 in that funding dried out, we have managed to survive, barely though.

We have come out much stronger and, during the whole of 2018, we worked tirelessly to ensure we have a programme that we cannot just sustain with overheads but that can ensure we generate our own income.

24 February 2019 marked the fifth year of our existence. We have come back with a vengeance and are here to stay.

NGO work is far from easy. One has to have tenacity and not be discouraged by the promises that often do not materialise.

What I have found in the NGO space is that, although most companies have CSI departments, if the programmes of the NGO do not match what the focus of their CSI is, you must just forget it.

You may think that since we are doing work in the health and education sector and because of my name it is easy to attract funds, but it is not. Despite the good intentions of most NGOs, it can be quite difficult to attract funding. One of the major reasons, in my view, is that for most companies and large organisations who give donor funding, their vetting system is mostly designed for large NPO/NGOs with a proven track record. It has taken us five years to find even kilter.

Back when I met Dr Liaqat Azam, around 2010, he asked me if there was a leadership programme that had been designed after Granddad's leadership qualities. I told him no and, when he asked me why, I could not give him an answer. He explained to me that Granddad was a visionary archetypal leader. I asked him to decode this for me and he did. Visionary archetypal leaders are authoritative as opposed to authoritarian or dictatorial. These leaders have the confidence to be led by a compelling vision and they do not seek to control those they work with. The visionary provides freedom to their colleagues to determine the best path to actualise the vision.

He further explained that this leadership programme could be an income-generating programme for the foundation, thus making its other programmes sustainable.

He then told me that the programme could be pitched to CEOs, top executives and such. I told him straight up that if and when I did agree to go ahead with it, the foundation would want to focus on the youth. I felt that it is much easier to mould the minds of the youth than adults. At a certain age, especially above the age of 21, one's identity is already crystallised.

To illustrate what I was talking about, I made an example about Granddad. Granddad grew up watching the tribal council in action. In fact, he confesses that it is the stories he listened to from Chief Zwelibhangile Joyi that drew him into politics.

Tatu Joyi would recount that, before the white people came, each clan lived in peace with other clans. According to legend, Zulus, Xhosas, Pondos and Thembus were all children of one father, but as the clans multiplied, they fell under the protection of district chiefs and each chief was the founding father of Isizwe (Nation), which came to be known after him. He further told Granddad (as recounted in Fatima Meer's *Higher than Hope* [1990]), 'They (whites) were few in numbers, but great in intrigue. They looked about for weaknesses in our tactics, they scratched our history and looked to see who quarrelled with whom in the past and who was quarrelling with whom presently and there, they poured poison and worked their witchcraft. They set brother against brother and while brothers fought, they took the land.'

Little did he know that political seeds were being planted in Granddad's mind. Because Granddad also watched tribal council and would see how the regent, Jongintaba, presided over it by listening to all the headmen from the villages, he developed a certain leadership style – consultative leadership.

You know when you are not ready for something, you find every reason to not do it? The idea that was being presented by Liaqat was no different. I simply was not ready for it.

In mid-2016 he approached me again and this time I was ready. My readiness was predominantly due to the floundering leadership in government and I knew I simply could not sit back and do nothing. Also, Pumla had shared with me that she was pregnant and the one thing I knew I never wanted to face was Nabeela asking me what I did when things got out of hand. Did I just talk about the state of affairs while sipping Champagne or sitting at an expensive restaurant and then go back to my life? That is how the Leading Like Mandela leadership framework came into being.

We partnered with the University of Johannesburg (UJ) and trained 100 students from five tertiary academic institutions. While we were training those students, I realised that leadership development should start much earlier. If you look at Granddad's leadership qualities, they were honed when he was still a young boy watching tribal council.

This leadership programme looks at intrinsic leadership rather than positional leadership. You cannot lead others if you cannot lead yourself.

We have since partnered with the UN and the United Nations Development Programme (UNDP) to start rolling out the programme. The Deputy Secretary-General, who gave a keynote speech at our official launch last December during the Mandela Centenary, emphasised how crucial it is, especially for Africa, to have good leaders. She also talked about the necessity of a certain kind of leadership to achieve the Sustainable Development Goals as part if the UN's 2030 Agenda for Sustainable Development.

As I am penning this book, the Thembekile Mandela Foundation, Public Service Commission (PSC), Moral Regeneration Movement and the UNDP have collaborated to host an intergenerational dialogue on ethical leadership. This intergenerational dialogue is also informed by the very first leadership five-day training we had at UJ. It has never been so clear to us that my generation and my children's generation are talking to each other.

Yes, we have come a long way as a foundation. As Granddad said in *Long Walk to Freedom*, 'After climbing one hill, one finds that there are many more hills to climb.'

I am truly excited by this next chapter of the foundation and the continuation of my passion.

Conclusion

I AM FIRST NDILEKA and then a Mandela.

I cannot say this enough. Throughout my life I have found that people tend to want to box me into just being the eldest grandchild of Evelyn Nomathamsanqa and Nelson Rolihlahla Mandela and being *only* their grandchild. I believe I have carved my own path, a path that was set when I was conceived by God. The Bible tells me that God knew me before I was even born and set a path for me to follow.

I have already spoken about how my identity was crystallised by the time Granddad was released. I am not denying that he had some influence in some of my decisions, but they are predominantly mine. For instance, Granddad wanted me to become a medical doctor, and I had wanted this too, but this was way before I even met him for the first time.

Around the time I was 14 or 15 years old and used to visit Mom in Durban, Daddy Phineas had a ritual he loved performing. He would summon us all to the living room and ask each of us to recite poems from school. I was never shy to show off back then and would recite a few. After that he would ask us what we wanted to become when we grew up. I would respond every time, in a heartbeat, that I wanted to become a doctor. I do not know where this wish or idea came from or what it was informed by; I just had it in my head.

I am sure I did share these wishes with Granddad because it is what he always wanted me to become. This was the subject of some of our major disagreements and fallouts when it did not happen. The point I am trying to make is that, had I been conformist in nature, I would have succumbed to the 'Mandela' notion and do what he wanted as the patriarch of my family.

Families like mine are quite imposing within their 'tribe' in the sense that at times you have to conform to the tribe rules or risk being a pariah. I mentioned this also in how my voice was drowned for the longest time until I found the courage to have it heard. In families like mine there are certain things that are not done and not said, not necessarily because they are bad, but because of what people may think. There are many families like that. I found this unwritten rule hard to conform to, which is why I have found myself at loggerheads with one or more members of my family at one time or the other.

I remember with amusement some time I had spent with one of Granddad's legal advisers back in the early 2000s. At that point, I was a pariah yet again. I can't remember exactly what had happened, but the legal adviser was teasing me about being in the dog box and we had a good laugh about it.

In my view, I have always done things because they made me feel good or resonated well with my soul. I have tried to be authentic to myself and not anyone else.

Since my increased activity on Facebook, people have tried to box me into the idea they have of my family and they are quickly learning I have my own voice. I need people to understand that when I express my opinion, I am expressing it as me, Ndileka, not a Mandela. Some try to shut me up by making analogies about Granddad or telling me that is not how he would behave or that is not what he would say.

Unless you have a valid point to argue or put across, be warned, do not try to emotionally blackmail me by mentioning him. My opinions are not informed by him but my experiences and my analysis of the situation. In fact, to do that is to insult my intelligence, as if I do not have a mind of my own.

This year we have experienced what I call 'silly season' – the period around elections – I found that where certain people were using my past statements for their own agendas. Take the statement I made that I would no longer vote sentimentally for the ANC. This is a statement I put on my Facebook timeline at the height of my frustration with the then Zuma administration, which was also around the time of the Life Esidimeni crisis and the SASSA/CPS saga.

I further qualified this statement when I was called by various media houses who wanted to talk about what I said.

What I really could not understand and still don't is how this became such a big deal. I have never been active in politics further than voting for the ANC in all past elections. What was stranger and more annoying was also being asked what my grandfather would say to my statement. There is nothing as condescending as being constantly compared to Granddad as if I do not have opinions of my own outside his ideologies. I was 52 years old at the time and you would expect people to know that, as a grown woman, I have my own ideas.

It's as if I cannot escape being in the shadow of my grandfather. That is one major reason I had to write this book, to talk about how I am my own person. Granddad was a colossus and I can never be like him. I am my own person with my own journey and purpose to fulfil.

Being in this family can be quite exhausting at times. I have had to read statements, sometimes toxic, from strangers who know nothing about me or my life, making suppositions they deem to be the truth. That is why I often feel empathy for the younger generation in my family. Over the years, I have perfected having a thick skin and vibrating on a higher frequency so that toxic people and their statements cannot reach me.

My faith and my yoga practice have made me resilient and authentic to my truth, my path and my story, without fear or favour. I thank Rundu for raising me to be a God-fearing woman. She taught me basic biblical principles of putting God first. I will not bow or curtsy to any person. I fear God and God alone. This strong belief in God has also carried me through the difficult phases of my life, when all human beings have fallen short. God carried me through all the challenging times I have mentioned in this book. He has brought angels to my life in the form of friends and various people who have assisted me, some by just listening and offering advice. I have learnt that sometimes all you need is someone who can listen to you unburden yourself. Even the judgemental people have helped me to grow.

Although Granddad was not really the religious type, from him I learnt how a relationship with God and faith are a sacred covenant. He never spoke publicly about religion or faith, yet I don't doubt that he had a sacred relationship with God. No person alive today can convince me that I do not have a relationship with God. Although my faith in God has never wavered, after my relationship with the Jehovah's Witnesses, I never really attended any formal church.

This, however, changed in 2015 after I had a debate with an ex-partner about religion. We had been dating for two years and he was a devout Catholic. He asked me one morning if I went to church and my response was in the negative. I told him I saw no need to go to church, as I read the Bible and prayed regularly. It was his response to my question of why he went to church that gave me food for thought. He told me he went to church for fellowship and to listen to the word of God from someone else's perspective. This, he said, was not to take that perspective as absolute, but to analyse it on his own and to understand it.

I must say, this made me think long and hard about my own beliefs about going to church. Shortly after this conversation, I decided to take a leap of faith and start attending regular church services. Since I had attended boarding schools with a strong leaning towards the Methodist Church and it was also the Mandela family church, I chose to attend at this denomination. In my quest for a spiritual home, I called my cousin Mandla to ask him if he knew any parishes I would be comfortable attending. He recommended the Glenferness Methodist Church led by Bishop Gary Rivas and his wife, Jacqui.

Mandla had given me their contact details and after calling and asking what time services were held, I attended my first church service a week before lent, and a week later I attended my very first lent service. I have loved this parish from my very first church service and I have never looked back. At last I have found a spiritual home and my faith has been freshly renewed.

From yoga, I have learnt the art of staying grounded in my truth, no matter what. More than being an exercise in discipline, weight loss and meditation, yoga has taught me how to accept myself in all my shortcomings. Done in a room full of mirrors, in a yoga class I come face to face with myself in all of my frailties. It has taught me to conquer my demons. There are postures that still challenge me, and it is particularly these postures that have taught me to accept that there are things I cannot control.

It has also taught me the ability to let go of things that

no longer serve me and the value in surrendering. It is when I have surrendered that things begin to shift for the better. Because yoga emphasises the importance of regular meditation it has taught me how to keep positive thoughts.

Granddad ends *Long Walk to Freedom* with this quote:

> *I have walked that long walk to freedom. I have tried not to falter. I have many missteps along the way. But I have discovered that after climbing a great hill, one only finds that there are many more hills to climb. I have taken a moment here to rest, to steal a view of the glorious vista that surrounds me, to look back at the distance I have come. But I can only rest only for a moment, for with freedom comes responsibilities and I dare not linger for my long walk has not ended yet.*

This book is me stealing a view at the glorious vista I have travelled. Like Granddad, I have walked a long road and have made many missteps and mistakes along the way. To those I have wronged consciously or unconsciously, may you all forgive me.

When I set out to put pen to paper, I wanted both my parents, Thoko and Thembi, and my grandmothers, Evelyn and Lilian, to take their rightful places in history, as I feel I have done. I honestly dare not linger. I now have a grandchild to mould and guide the same way I was guided and moulded by my grandmothers.

I have also finally laid my ghosts to rest, although I know the nature of ghosts is such that they do creep up time and again, but I shall be ready to tackle them head on when they do.

I am Ndileka Mandela, the first of the first of the first. This is my story and I am sticking to it.

Acknowledgements

MY JOURNEY INTO SELF-DISCOVERY began when I turned 40, but my real journey of coming to terms with my position in my family started with Tembeka Khaka, for it was she who first told me I was the first of the first of the first. Her statement helped me refocus my life and from then on my purpose began to unfold.

There are many people I would like to acknowledge. One of those people is my aunt Maki and her husband, my uncle Dr Isaac Amuah. Aunt Maki was a great influence in my life, especially during my teenage years. Through her, I began a love affair with reading, which I still have to this day and this I passed on to my daughter, Pumla. Uncle Ike (as we all call Dr Amuah) introduced me to the love of classical music.

The list of people I would like to acknowledge is vast. Thanks to Mama Graça who became both a mother and a grandmother to me when the two were no more. I will never forget the day I went to our home in Houghton to tell her about starting the Thembekile Mandela Foundation and she said to me: 'Darling you have done what Papa and I could not do, you have given Thembi a face.' Little did she know what these words meant to me and what a source of encouragement they have been since then.

Many thanks to the Nelson Mandela Foundation for opening their archives for me to have access to and use most of the material pertaining to my father in the letters that Grandad wrote to various people around the time Dad died. These letters have allowed me to gain perspective as to the depth of pain and the sense of loss Grandad felt after Dad died. These letters not only provided a source of information, but I hope they will be able to start to give my sister Nandi an idea of what she missed, and our children of who their grandfather was.

Verne Harris, thank you for pestering me to put pen to paper and nudging me ever so gently, in the only way you know how. Sahm Venter, thank you for being the first to send me all the information pertaining to Dad.

To my many cousins I grew up with, you also took part in shaping who I have become. Thank you for all the quirky times in Cofimvaba, Engcobo and Qunu.

Thank you to my publisher, Jacana Media, with specific reference to Neilwe Mashigo. We clicked from our very first meeting after being introduced by Stephen Miyambu. Thank you to Masego Panyane for assisting in putting my words into a story format. Thank you to Linda, my editor from Jacana, although at times you did split hairs!

Last but not least, I would like to thank the team in Touwsrivier who were instrumental in the erecting of the first and only existing monument in the memory of my father, Thembekile Madiba Mandela, with the exception of his grave, that is. The people I would like to acknowledge are Touwsrivier Heritage and Conservation Society in co-operation with the Touwsrivier Tourism Association and the Breede Valley Municipality.

Thank you to my public family as well, as over the years, when I would share titbits of my life, they would encourage me to write, and I finally did.

Finally, although this is not an acknowledgement but a note to my granddaughter, Nabeela Thokozile Mandela – Nana: Nana, I thank your parents for creating you. You have changed my life in ways I can never articulate. This is an authentic story of my life as told by me, your grandmother, which will outlive me. You are growing up exactly how I grew up, being brought up by my gogo, as you call me. I hope you will cherish the values that were instilled in me and which I have shared here. I hope when you get older and read you can get to know my parents and my grandparents, through my eyes as well.

This is my narrative and to time infinite it will remain so.